LOST FOR WORDS

DYSLEXIA AT SECOND-LEVEL AND BEYOND

A PRACTICAL GUIDE FOR PARENTS AND TEACHERS

WYN MCCORMACK

ISBN 0 9532427 0 6

Cover Design   Caslon & Co
Printed by   ColourBooks Ltd., Baldoyle, Dublin 13
Published by   Tower Press - Stillorgan, 3 Priory Drive, Blackrock, Co. Dublin
Typeset by   Carole Lynch, 52 Seapark, Mt Prospect Avenue, Clontarf, Dublin 3

To Robin and Simon who have worked with such perseverance against the odds over the years and who have taught me so much

Table of Contents

Glossary of Terminology

ACLD	Association for Children and Adults with Learning Difficulties.
CAO	Central applications system for Universities, Regional Technical Colleges, Institutes of Technology and other colleges.
CERT	State agency for training in the hotel, catering and tourism industry.
CIT	Cork Institute of Technology.
DIT	Dublin Institute of Technology comprising of the College of Commerce, Aungier Street; Colleges of Technology, Kevin Street and Bolton Street; College of Marketing and Design, Mountjoy Square; College of Catering, Cathal Brugha Street and the College of Music.
ESRI	Economic and Social Research Institute.
LCAP	Leaving Certificate Applied Programme.
LCVP	Leaving Certificate Vocational Programme
NCEA	National Council for Educational Awards which gives accreditation to national degree, diploma and certificate courses in Institutes of Technology, Regional Technical Colleges and some private college courses.
NCVA	National Council for Vocational Awards which gives accreditation to Post Leaving Certificate courses.
NTDI	National Training and Development Institute.
NCIR	National College of Industrial Relations.
NUI	National University of Ireland, comprising of
	UCD, University College, Dublin,
	UCC, University College, Cork,
	UCG, University College, Galway,
	St. Patrick's College, Maynooth.
NCAD	National College of Art and Design.

PLC	Post Leaving Certificate courses.
RTC	Regional Technical College.
UCAS	Centralised application system for degree and diploma courses in U.K.
WIT	Waterford Institute of Technology.

Introduction

The origins of this book lie in the journey of discovery I have taken since 1985 when it was confirmed that our twin sons, Robin and Simon, had a learning difficulty. It was a journey that began in ignorance. In spite of the fact that I was a secondary teacher, I knew little about the subject of dyslexia at that time. Although I received help from teachers, psychologists and ACLD (the Association for Children and Adults with Learning Difficulties), it was a journey taken for the most part on my own as I tried, over the years, to assess what exactly were the twins' difficulties, what techniques worked best for them and what resources were available to them. In recent years I have met with parents soon after a child was similarly diagnosed and have heard the same questions being asked and have seen these parents starting out on the same path searching for the same information.

My primary objective in writing this book is a hope that it will be a source of relevant information for parents of dyslexic children.

At the time that the twins were diagnosed, I was fortunate in that I was working as a guidance counsellor, as indeed, I still am. My role as a guidance counsellor puts me in a central place in the school system where I have access to information relevant to their needs. I deal with the vocational, educational and personal counselling needs of students from the ages of twelve to eighteen. I am involved, among other things, as a member of a team looking after the needs of students with specific learning difficulties. I receive copies of psychological reports on such students and I refer parents of students to psychologists. I keep up-to-date with the trends in employment and educational courses available after second-level. This is a rapidly changing field with more flexibility entering into the routes to qualifications. This flexibility can be particularly important for dyslexic students. During the years my roles, both as a teacher and guidance counsellor, have been of great benefit to the twins and the corollary of this is that I have become much more aware of dyslexia and the problems dyslexics face in second-level education.

A second objective in writing this book is to increase the awareness of the needs of such students in the public mind and, in particular, the teaching profession. While there has been some progress in recent years, much more is needed. In the last three years I have personally known ten students who were not diagnosed until their mid-teens. They had passed through primary school and partially through second-level without teachers identifying their difficulties. Certainly they have met with failure and their confidence and self-esteem have been affected greatly by such a late diagnosis. It is my belief that there are many such undiagnosed SLD students in Irish schools.

I will be referring to the twins, Robin and Simon, and the techniques which worked for them and some that did not throughout this book, so it may be helpful to give a brief introduction to them, our family history and to explain how the dyslexia has affected them.

They were our first children and were already showing some signs of difficulty at the age of two to three. They were slow to talk. We attributed some of this to 'Twintalk', which is that they were so busy communicating between themselves that it slowed down their language development. They also found sequences difficult to remember and they tended to be clumsy. They did not tie shoelaces until they were nine and rode a bike for the first time at the age of ten. In their early years at school they found order and pattern difficult and they repeated a year. As they had started school at four years and ten months, this made them old for their class.

On the basis of a psychological assessment, we were fortunate to get them a place in St. Oliver Plunkett's School in Monkstown when they were eight. St. Oliver Plunkett's is a primary school which was established to provide specialised tuition for pupils who have reading difficulties. The twins spent two years there. They went back into fourth class in Carysfort National School but, since their reading was still three to four years behind, they had considerable difficulties with the primary school curriculum. We applied for and received an exemption from Irish from the Department of Education. This helped. It had been hard to see them struggling to learn the sounds in English and then having to learn different sounds for the same letters in Irish. During the years in Carysfort they attended ACLD Saturday morning classes and also attended summer school. It is much to their credit that they tackled all this extra work with perseverance. Towards the end of their years in primary school, their reading developed and this opened the way to making progress in school.

After much research about second-level schools, we decided to send them to St. Gerard's, Bray, for their secondary schooling. Here, provided they received help at home with notes for the different subjects, they coped well. As this was one of the early years of the Junior Certificate course, there were no revision handbooks available, so it was a question of summarising the books ourselves. For the first time they were participating fully in class and received great affirmation when they passed class exams and tests.

They continued to need help with notes during the three years of their Junior Certificate course and also needed help with goal-setting and organisation of work. They attended the examination preparation classes run by ACLD. They both were delighted to receive three honours grades on honours papers in the Junior Certificate and good passes in their other subjects. This gave an enormous boost to their confidence and it showed how far they had journeyed since learning to read at the age of ten/eleven.

They still have difficulties with spelling and with structuring written answers. I can never see them spelling well but they use a word-processor with a spell-check.

Robin and Simon are still heavily reliant on notes being supplied to them. They are now in senior cycle and their next goals are the Leaving Certificate in 1998 and their career choices afterwards.

During these years my husband, Tom, and myself decided early on that I was more suited to work with the twins as I am a teacher. Part of the reason I was able to work with the boys is their co-operative and pleasant personalities and their desire to achieve. Together we formed a very compatible work team (for the most part). At times progress was infuriatingly slow; at times impatience set in. I learnt to recognise when, as a result of being too tired, I became more edgy and far more critical. A difficulty which might have been laughed at in September could be the basis for a row in February when we were much more fatigued. I learnt to deliberately avoid confronting issues when under stress. To give out about school work on some occasions would be detrimental to the other work we had put in on self-esteem and confidence. We wanted Robin and Simon to feel home was a refuge and that our love was not conditional on school performance.

Together as a family we have shared moments of great exhilaration and satisfaction at their achievements, such as their Junior Certificate results, doing the An Gaisce Awards at bronze and silver level and their participation in the Young Scientist Competition.

Because there was a gap of six years between the twins and their brother Tom, it meant we were able to give them more attention than might be possible in a family situation where the siblings are closer together in age. It also meant they had very little competition inside the family. In some families it can increase pressure on the dyslexic student when younger brothers and sisters overtake their achievements in school tasks such as reading and writing. Soon after Tom died in infancy, the youngest member of the family, Ted, was born in 1986. He is minimally affected by dyslexia. We were conscious of the fact that dyslexia can run in families and had become aware of adult members in the family who have dyslexic characteristics. From the beginning we had been on the look-out for indicators that Ted might be dyslexic but because he was a very articulate, logical child with good co-ordination, we had felt there was no problem.

However, by first class, we discovered he was memorising the content of his readers, so it appeared as though he could read but in reality he had no grasp of reading. He was assessed by a psychologist and his profile showed uneven abilities with exceptional strengths in the logical and mathematical areas, average ability in verbal skills and below average spelling. He received intensive remedial intervention that year and it had dramatic effects. His reading is now well above average and he is making good progress in school. There is a residual spelling difficulty and learning Irish remains hard work.

He is a good example of how early intervention can minimise the effects of dyslexia in some students.

During these years we have spent many hundreds of pounds, if not thousands, on the three boys. Assessments and extra tuition are major costs. We received no financial help from the State. I strongly suggest that these costs should be at least tax deductible. Medical costs are tax deductible. Why not the costs of a psychological assessment? If the psychological assessment suggests the student needs one-to-one tuition or summer tuition, why not these costs as well?

We realise we have been fortunate in benefiting from the support services which are provided by the Department of Education and Science. Robin and Simon received on-going remedial help in school; they went to St. Oliver Plunkett's School for two years; they received an exemption from Irish from fourth class on and they have special arrangements in state examinations. Not all dyslexic students have the same access to such facilities.

Over the years we have received great help.

Robin and Simon attended:

Mount Anville National School, Kilmacud,

St. Oliver Plunkett's School, Monkstown,

Carysfort National School, Blackrock and are at present attending St. Gerard's, Bray.

Ted is attending Scoil San Treasa, Mount Merrion.

The staff of all these schools have always been most co-operative and positive and have done their utmost to meet the boys' needs. They have listened and tried to facilitate our requests. Our thanks to all the teachers concerned. In particular thanks are due to the Headmaster and staff of St. Gerard's where Robin and Simon have attended for the whole of their secondary schooling.

ACLD has been a font of information. Their newsletters and lectures have helped us to understand what dyslexia is and how it affects students. I have attended their lectures and conferences. Over the years the boys have attended their Saturday School and exam preparation classes. Parents of children with learning difficulties should become members of this organisation. It is a great support to talk to other parents of dyslexic students, to share information and to feel that one is not struggling alone.

My colleagues in St. David's Secondary School, Greystones, have given me great advice and instructed me in their own particular subjects so that I could help with the twins' homework, as well as listening and giving me constant encouragement.

Much thanks are due to two friends, Pamela McAree, who did trojan work editing this manuscript and my colleague, Cairbre O Ciardha, who gave me advice and suggestions.

I hope that my book will pass on some of the insights I have gained and that it will help dyslexics, their parents and their teachers to understand how dyslexia can affect students at second-level and what can be done to help them overcome their difficulties. I also hope that it might raise public awareness. If teachers, parents and the general public are more aware that such problems exist, it will lead to earlier identification and to more facilities and support systems being provided.

Dyslexia at Second-Level and Beyond

2

My knowledge about dyslexia results from my own practical experience as a teacher, a guidance counsellor and, most important of all, a parent. From the time my husband and I became aware that Robin and Simon had a learning difficulty, I have read many books and attended courses to further my knowledge. So when I describe dyslexia it is with knowledge gleaned from the books I have read, from seminars I have attended and from practical experience in the school and at home.

While I try to give an overall description of dyslexia, I am looking in particular at the way dyslexia can affect a student at second-level and beyond. This is the sector of education in which I work and have experience.

Dyslexia is usually diagnosed by an educational psychologist who identifies marked under-achievement in language skills in comparison with a student's level of intelligence. The word itself comes from the Greek meaning 'difficulty with words or language'. International figures show it occurs in about 4% to 8% of the population in varying degrees and with varying effects. As yet reported figures are far lower in Ireland (see Chap. 5). As dyslexia is a very imprecise term, the term Specific Learning Difficulty (SLD) is also used. This term reflects the fact that the range of dyslexic characteristics is so diverse and dyslexic students may not suffer from the same characteristics or to the same extent. The profile of the student's strengths and weaknesses and the causes of these weaknesses is unique and specific to that student. The term dyslexia is more widely known but I will use both terms from now on.

In 1991 research by Pumfrey and Reason in the U.K. showed that 87% of psychologists preferred the term specific learning difficulty and only 30% thought the word dyslexia useful. My own opinion favoured the term SLD originally. However there has been a widening of the meaning of the phrase 'learning difficulty', with the growth of kinder terms for educationally handicapped children. The precise meaning of the term is often not clear. At least the public has some concept of what the word dyslexia means.

Pollock & Waller in their book *Day-to-day Dyslexia in the Classroom* refer to the fact that in the United States the term learning disabled is used. This can be shortened to LD which is beginning to be accepted as 'learning different'. This is a far more positive term. It takes into account that every one of us has learning difficulties in some form or another. Some people can be excellent readers but have difficulty in Maths or in understanding machines. The SLD student is unfortunate in that his learning difficulties are centred on skills that are so critical to school achievement and where it is so obvious when a child fails.

Since more boys than girls are affected by dyslexia, to improve the flow of the text, I refer to the student as a 'he' throughout in preference to the more clumsy he/she. Of course, all I say refers equally to girls. When I refer to an organisation, its address is given under the heading 'Useful Addresses' at the back of the book.

Dyslexia is not related to low intelligence. Generally it is true to say that intelligence and reading ability are strongly linked. SLD students are different. Intelligence and language skills are not correlated for them. There are plenty of cases of highly intelligent students who had difficulty picking up written language skills. Some of the historical figures of which this was true are Einstein, Edison, Yeats, Leonardo Da Vinci and Rodin.

While psychologists are not sure as to the causes of SLD, there is evidence of a genetic component. In March 1996 I attended the AGM of the Association for Children and Adults with Learning Difficulties, at which Mr. T. Pottage from the British Dyslexia Association spoke on the advantages of computers for dyslexics. Mr. Pottage, who has a dyslexic son, made the comment that dyslexia is often inherited. Parents inherit it from their children! It is only since his son was diagnosed that he has recognised some of the effects of dyslexia in himself. The same is true of myself. I had no difficulties at school and went on to third-level education. However now I recognise that I do have some difficulties. I can never tell right from left and I transpose letters and numbers. My own family history would lend itself to the argument that there is a genetic component in dyslexia. My brother was diagnosed as dyslexic in his mid-teens and my three sons are all affected to some extent. Robin and Simon would lend even stronger evidence to a genetic component. They are identical twins and, in their difficulties with languages, have mirrored each other. At the time they were learning to read, they made exactly the same mistakes. 'Saw' became 'was' and 'on' became 'no' for both of them. Even now, when writing, they make similar spelling mistakes. If there is a history of SLD in a family, parents should be on the look-out for indicators that a child may be affected. The earlier the child gets help, the less the damage to self-esteem.

Happily there are now screening tests which can point to possible problems for the child from the age of four. These became available in 1996. The DEST (Dyslexia Early Screening Test) has been developed at the University of Sheffield and trials of this test have been held by the Psychology Department in Trinity College, Dublin. This test is now available from ETC Consult. CoPS (Cognitive Profiling System) is another test to screen for dyslexic characteristics in the four to six age group. It has been developed at the University of Hull. It measures the child's reaction to various challenges on a computer screen.

There has also been progress on screening tests for the older students. The Dyslexia Screening Test (DST) has also been developed at the University of Sheffield for use with students from 6 years and 6 months to the age of 16 years and 5 months. It is also available from ETC Consult. Another screening instrument has recently been developed for students in third-level education and adult education by Dorota Zdzienskil, with the support of the University of Leicester and the University of Ulster. While it has been created specifically to identify the dyslexic student, it also investigates individual learning styles and study habits. Further information on it is available from Interactive Services Limited.

Up until the development of these screening tests, the earliest a child would be assessed was at age seven or eight. The reason for the assessment would be worries over the child's achievement in school. The child would already be failing. If screening tests can point to SLD at the age of four or five, before the child has fallen behind, help can be given earlier and the difficulty may not become so acute. Importantly, if a child has to wait until seven or eight to be diagnosed and is already falling behind, his self-esteem is already being affected. This will compound the difficulties for the child. Afraid of appearing to fail, children can become experts in avoiding tasks that they do badly. Evasion tactics used can be psychosomatic illnesses, acting up, tantrums or becoming the class clown. They can give up trying, as it can be preferable to fail by not working at a subject rather than not being able to do it. This can continue through secondary schooling.

By the time students arrive at secondary school at the age of twelve approximately, most SLD students are able to read to some extent. If they have been lucky enough to have been diagnosed early, they may have received some remedial/resource teaching. Some may have attended ACLD workshops or have had extra tuition on a one-to-one basis. Indeed, if students cannot read by this stage, they will have major and serious problems managing the second-level curriculum.

Many people believe that dyslexia is a problem with reading and that if the student learns to read the problem is solved. However what must be remembered is the huge variety in the range and extent of the difficulties experienced by SLD students. Each SLD student has his own unique profile of strengths and weaknesses. At second-level, SLD students could experience difficulty in one or some of the following:

READING

Most SLD students are able to read by the time they reach second-level. However the reading may be laboured or be affected by pressure of time or complicated texts. They can be slow at reading and can misread some words. They possibly confuse letters and sequences. They can concentrate so much on deciphering the text that they can lose comprehension. They may have to re-read a page to make sense of it. It can take them longer than other students to find a word or passage on a page. Even if they can read quite fluently, they may dislike reading aloud. In the pressure of an exam a SLD student, who can read quite well, is still quite liable to misread a question as stress can exacerbate dyslexic symptoms.

When students start at second-level, their textbooks can be quite daunting. The texts are usually geared for the three years of the Junior Certificate course and many of the texts use the language suitable for students of fourteen or fifteen. This does not help the SLD student. He can find it difficult to pick out the main points and summarise the material in the textbooks. This skill is critical to success at second-level where the student has to be familiar with so much information. He can also have difficulty when using reference material in picking out the relevant points he wants and so become flooded with information.

SPELLING

Whereas most SLD students will have achieved some level of reading skills by the time of entry to second-level, spelling difficulties tend to persist for a longer period. SLD students may not perceive the sequences or patterns that letters make to form words. They can lack the visual memory of words. Many people spell well because they remember the visual shape of a word.

They become aware if the word "looks" wrong. Many SLD students do not have this memory. Typical errors include:

transposing letters, e.g. hostipal for hospital,

letter confusion, d/b, p/q and m/w being mistaken for each other,

omission of letters or endings e.g. spraind for sprained,

phonetic spelling, e.g. kawphy for coffee,

impossible combinations of letters e.g. qiet,

inconsistent spelling where the same word is spelt several ways,

adding or deleting syllables or vowels, e.g. rember for remember.

If they take the time to try to spell correctly, it can slow down the writing process and interfere with the flow of ideas. Sometimes they try to avoid a word they cannot spell and seek an alternative. This can sound stilted and interrupt the flow of language. Some may mispronounce words which can have dire consequences for spelling.

HANDWRITING

Handwriting can be difficult to read and badly formed. This may be the result of directional confusion and/or poor motor visual skills. Directional confusion affects concepts such as up/down, left/right, top/bottom. The student, when beginning to learn to write, does not know which way the pen should go. A video produced by the Eagle Hill School, Connecticut, tries to give parents, teachers and psychologists some insight into the difficulties faced by the SLD student. There is an exercise to illustrate directional confusion. A mirror is set on a desk and a person is asked to trace over a pattern but can look only into the reversed image on the mirror. Try this one out yourself and it will give you some appreciation of how difficult some students find the task of orientation.

NOTE-TAKING

Many SLD students face difficulties in taking notes either from the blackboard or in a lecture. Poor motor visual skills mean they find it difficult to combine looking at the board, copying into their notebook and then looking up to find the right place to continue. Visual memory problems mean they may take fewer words down from the board each time and so are looking back to the board more often. In a lecture some students may have to concentrate fully on what is being said in order to understand it. It is as though they have to translate it to make sense of it. The direct connection where a student can take down what a lecturer is saying and write simultaneously may not apply. This slows them down. If faced with words they cannot visualise and so cannot spell, they can come to a halt and so miss whatever is said next. Besides the problems of taking down notes, the finished copy is likely to be difficult to read and to study from because of poor handwriting and misspellings.

PRESENTATION OF WORK

Their work can be difficult to correct because of poor handwriting, poor or bizarre spelling and lack of layout on the page. Spacing of work, margins and headings do not come naturally to some dyslexics. They can lose marks because teachers cannot decipher what they have written. It can also take far longer to correct. Teachers can sometimes judge students on the appearance of their work. If the work is very untidy and disorganised, assumptions may be made about the content with the consequence of lower marks.

VERBAL EXPRESSION

Some SLD students have difficulty finding the correct name for a familiar object. They know all about the object and what it does but the recall of the exact term eludes them. They may resort to 'you know what I mean' or 'thingamijig'. When learning history, they may know the causes, course and results of an historical event such as the Reformation but the names of the people, events and places are difficult to remember. When attempting to explain something at length, they can lack organisation and structure. They may know what they want to say but they do not start with a beginning, go on to a middle and thence to a conclusion. It can be very mixed up.

WRITTEN EXPRESSION

While SLD students may be familiar with a topic and have plenty of ideas, their written answers may lack planning and structure, so the points they wish to make are not clearly represented. Writing can be a cumbersome task and one which SLD students may wish to avoid. Answers may be far too short, points may be left undeveloped. Sentence construction and punctuation can cause difficulties in clarity and precision of writing.

SEQUENCING

Sequencing plays a part in some of the other difficulties listed in this section. However it deserves to be mentioned separately because sequencing information is so important at second-level. Poor sequential skills can affect a student in some of the following ways:

◆ He may not perceive the day-to-day sequences that most people take for granted such as the days of the week or the months of the year. This can make planning homework and revision difficult. The teacher may feel he has communicated clearly his instructions to the class but the SLD student does not share the same concept of the time scale and so misinterprets what the teacher has said.

◆ If the student is given a task of learning a sequence off-by-heart such as poetry, he may find it virtually impossible as he will confuse the sequence. For this reason some SLD students find it difficult to tell jokes. They can mix-up the punchline and ruin the joke. If this happens with jokes, how much more difficult is it to learn a long poem?

◆ When given a question either orally or in writing, he may find it difficult to sequence his answer. This can mean that although he may know a lot of information, he cannot find the means to express it in a clearly structured way.

MATHS

In Maths SLD students may have difficulty in remembering sequences such as tables which can slow down calculations or the sequence of the steps to be followed in a long question. They may also take longer to distinguish between symbols such as +, -, and < >. They may not grasp the distinction between words with exact meanings such as minus, subtraction and reduction. Small link words, which the SLD student may overlook, can change the meaning of an instruction leaving the student confused, e.g. six *by* six, six *times* six, six *into* six, six sixes, six *plus* six and six *and* six. In a verbally expressed question it can be the English in the question and not the mathematical concept that they do not understand. In Maths the student usually works from right to left, which is opposite to the way words are read. This can add to the difficulties. Poor layout and presentation can mean answers are wrong even if the method is correct. In a timed oral test the student may need to decode the question to understand what he is being asked to do and so misses the next question and falls behind.

DIRECTIONAL CONFUSION

This has been mentioned under handwriting but it can affect students in other aspects of the school curriculum. They may find it difficult to tell left from right, read maps, have difficulty finding their way about and remembering routes. In Physical Education or in other subjects where they have to follow a certain action, they may have to translate the action into instructions in their mind as to what their limbs should do. They do not automatically know which arm or leg to use.

FOLLOWING INSTRUCTIONS

The SLD student may have difficulty following verbal instructions if more than one instruction is given at a time, particularly if direction or sequences are included. If the teacher gives an instruction such as 'When you have finished your work, and taken down your homework from the board, you may leave', the SLD student may register the last piece and leave immediately. This can get him into trouble in school.

Orally given details of school events may lack some essential detail by the time it reaches home and parents. An example may be the notice about a Parents' Night Meeting. By the time it reaches home, the date or the time or the venue may have been forgotten or confused.

LACK OF CONFIDENCE

The SLD student may experience a few or many of the difficulties mentioned above. However a very common result of having dyslexia is lack of confidence or low self-esteem. The student has experienced failure. He is aware that he does not make the same progress as his peers. It can make him reluctant to ask questions in class. He tries to avoid answering questions in case the answer he gives is wrong. Reading aloud can be embarrassing. He has faced frustration in not being able to do tasks set by the teacher. Being in a classroom is a source of anxiety and tension to him. He may avoid new challenges so as to avoid further failure. He can lack the confidence in his ability to achieve. He may give up trying. This lack of confidence can permeate the whole of his schooling and even affect sports and hobbies. He may be embarrassed by his problem and be reluctant to tell other students that he is dyslexic. Under stress, such as in an exam, dyslexic characteristics can be exacerbated and tasks, previously managed well, become more difficult.

Again it must be stressed that each SLD student is affected in varying ways. Some may have reading and spelling problems, for others it may be sequencing and structure. Some may be affected minimally, others severely. Teachers and school authorities need to know the profile of the individual student. The psychological report gives valuable information and suggestions. Parents should be consulted and listened to. They have the inside track on the difficulties faced by the student and ideas on what strategies work best in the effort to help him achieve his potential. Because parents are the main decision-makers for the student, I have been surprised to discover incidences where they did not have access to a copy of the psychological report. If they attend a psychologist privately, they receive a copy. These reports can be invaluable when parents are talking to teachers. The reports help establish the precise difficulties for the student and can form the basis for making critical decisions on educational choices.

For reasons that are still unclear, reading through coloured lenses can help some students to perceive reading material and process it correctly. Dr. H. Irlen gave this theory the name Scotopic Sensitivity. It is possible for a student to be tested in Ireland to see if coloured lenses will help the student perceive the written word better.

Educational Kinesiology is another and relatively new form of therapy, which, it is claimed, can help dyslexic students. Kinesiologists look at how the body's various functions are balanced and integrated. The brain is divided into two hemispheres; the left hemisphere is concerned with logical, rational and scientific abilities. This is where language is mainly processed. The right hemisphere is concerned with artistic, intuitive, visual and spatial skills. It is suggested by many specialists in the field of dyslexia that difficulties arise when the language areas are split more evenly between the two hemispheres. Kinesiologists suggest a range of exercises and massages aimed towards whole brain learning through movement repatterning.

Some parents fear that when the student knows he has dyslexia, the label will encourage him to do less as he has an excuse for not learning. I do not agree with this view. Many students feel a sense of relief. The diagnosis of a specific learning difficulty explains their lack of achievement in school and it can encourage them to make an effort provided the tasks are geared to their abilities. One student voiced his relief that there was 'nothing wrong in his head'. Another student was not diagnosed until he was in third year. Up to this point he had been extremely disruptive and it was very likely he would be asked not to return to senior cycle. Once the diagnosis was made, he changed remarkably. He not only passed his Leaving Certificate, but also was in the running to be considered for Student of the Year at the end of his final year in the school.

There is research to show the dyslexic profile of abilities can contain strengths. Many of these students may be strong in logical reasoning which may lead to success in mastering computers. They are good at constructional tasks such as building Lego or Meccano. Spatial Relations (the ability to visualise in three dimensions) can be a strength. In a video on dyslexia produced for the BBC programme QED, Tom West, an author who has written several books on dyslexia, suggests that dyslexia is a very positive asset in today's and tomorrow's world and that very good visual spatial relations skills may be more appropriate to a new world rather than the old skills based on words. Humdrum tasks such as spelling and sums can be left to computers. These were the skills of the medieval monks. Tom West has written a book called *In the Mind's Eye* which profiles a number of gifted individuals such as Faraday and Einstein, all of whom had some literacy or numeracy difficulties during their school career and later as adults.

Choosing a Second-Level School 3

Deciding which second-level school would be the most suitable for a dyslexic student is a key decision for parents. Some parents may not have a choice since there may be only one school for the area. Other parents have a choice particularly in city areas.

To make the best choice, the parents of a SLD student need to have as much information as possible about the schools and what they offer. Below are some points to consider when choosing a school. Some of this information will be freely available in school literature. Some may be available on request from the school. Parents of students already in the school can also be a source of information.

CLASS PLACEMENT

How does the school place students in classes? Most schools have more than one class in each year group. Different ways to place students in classes include:

Mixed ability

The class is made up of students from all ability levels. If a school is taking in one hundred and twenty students, the students are randomly broken into 4 different groups of thirty.

Proponents of mixed ability say that it avoids labelling students as failures because they did not get into a higher class and that placement in a bottom class can have a detrimental effect on self-esteem and motivation, a consequence being that students can give up and stop making an effort to achieve. On the other hand some teachers say it is very difficult to teach mixed ability classes and that better progress is made if the class has the same ability level. A mixed ability system favours the SLD student. It means he is in a class where he will benefit from the wide range of ideas and discussions. He may be able to use his strong abilities in the class room, for example in debate or class discussion, while at the same time the teacher knows of his weaker writing skills.

Setting
This means that instead of an overall assessment incoming students are assessed in an individual subject, e.g. Irish, English and Maths. The students are placed in class on their ability in that subject. A student could be in the top Maths class but a middle English class. This type of placement takes a lot of school resources because all the classes in a particular subject must be held at the same time. If there are one hundred and twenty students in a year group, a school will need four Maths teachers available at the same time. Setting can be of benefit for a dyslexic student, as it can take into account his strengths. However, if he is placed in a weak English class because of his verbal skills, although these skills may benefit from the slower pace set by teachers, he may miss the stimulation and ideas which would be present in a mixed ability class.

Streaming
This is where students are placed in classes by their performance at assessment. In the case of one hundred and twenty students, the first thirty could be in the highest stream, the next thirty in the second stream and so on. The class is together for core subjects, typically Irish, English, Maths, Religion, History and Geography.

Streaming is criticised for the effect it can have on student morale. Students may end up in a lower stream for many reasons. Family problems, lack of support at home for schooling or disruptive behaviour can contribute to poor academic achievement. These problems may spill over into class interactions. In an ideal classroom, the teacher is likely to make more progress if the class is at the same ability level. However, while this may be true of top streams, many other factors such as the problems mentioned above can affect the progress in a weak stream. This is probably the least attractive scenario for a SLD student with average or above average ability. The entrance assessment is not likely to show his strengths and unless the psychological assessment is taken into account, he can be placed in a class which will improve on basic skills but will not provide the challenge, stimulus and verbal discussion of which he is capable. He may become bored at the slow pace of the class.

There is one very important point about streaming to consider particularly in relation to a dyslexic student. Take a student who has very weak verbal skills and very good Maths. If the student is placed in a lower stream on account on the poor verbal skills, will it deprive the student of sitting higher level Maths in the Junior Certificate? In some schools this may be possible. The student may be placed in a lower stream class and as a consequence will sit ordinary or foundation level Irish, English and Maths in state examinations. If parents are aware that the student has this profile with strong Maths, they should check this point at the time the student enters second-level. It is too late to discover the student is taking ordinary level Maths at the end of first year or during second year. The student, by then, will have fallen behind the pace of an honours Maths class. Parents should also be aware of the format of the entrance assessment. A reading test will give a indication of the student's ability to read, a spelling test will give an indication of his ability to spell but a Maths test, where the questions are verbally put, may be more a test of the student's ability to understand English rather than Maths and may not give an accurate indication of the student's skills in Maths.

Banding

This is an attempt to merge mixed ability and strict streaming. With 120 students, the top sixty students on assessment would be grouped into one band. Two classes would be formed from this group randomly. The weaker sixty students on assessment would be the second band and again two classes would be formed. It means there is no bottom class. Banding reduces some of the negative effects of streaming.

Overall my opinion is that mixed ability or setting best meets the needs of most dyslexic students.

CHOICE OF SUBJECTS

Parents of SLD students face the major decision of subject choice when the students begin second-level. This decision can be far more important for SLD students than for other students as there may be subjects in which these students will not succeed no matter how hard they try and other subjects in which they can make good progress.

Some schools offer a wide choice of Junior and Leaving Certificate subjects while in other schools the choice is more restricted. The subjects on offer depend on the school's resources and the number of pupils attending the school.

A small number of schools have the structure that in the course of first year the student has classes in all the subjects on offer and the decision about subject choice is made at the end of that year. This allows a more informed decision to be made as the student knows how he has achieved in each subject. More typically the parents and student have to choose subjects when the student is entering second-level.

Students following the Junior Certificate programme in a secondary school must take Irish, English, Maths, History, Geography and CSPE (Civic, Social and Political Education). Normally they choose three or four additional subjects called options. The most commonly available options are Art, Business Studies, Home Economics, Languages, Metalwork, Materials Technology, Science and Technical Graphics. There are other subjects in the Junior Certificate examination which a small number of pupils take such as Technology, Music, Classical Studies, Environmental/ Social Studies and Typewriting.

In some option subjects there can be a limit on the number of places due to teacher availability or a maximum class size restriction. The school will have a system for allocating places to such classes. In my own school it is in order of application for option classes. For some dyslexic students option choice may be critical. There may be some subjects they will enjoy and do well and other subjects in which they will find it difficult to make progress whereas a student not affected by dyslexia may achieve equally well in all subjects. When a student has a number of subjects he enjoys, it can change his whole attitude to school. Parents should ask well in advance how places in option classes are allocated. In some cases, because of the importance of the student studying the most appropriate subjects, a case for positive discrimination in allocating option places could be made. It would be helpful if such a suggestion is contained in the student's psychological report.

Most students will take eight or nine subjects in the Junior Certificate. For some severely affected SLD students, this may be a particularly heavy burden. The option structure may provide a way to reduce the number of subjects being taken. This is how it could work. The student will have core subjects such as English, Maths, History, CSPE, Geography and Irish (unless the student is exempt from Irish). The possible option structure offered by a school might be that the student takes one subject from each of the following lines, giving him four option subjects.

1. French, Art, Business Studies
2. Science, Business Studies, Home Economics, German

3. Science, Materials Technology, Technical Graphics, Business Studies
4. Art, Science, Home Economics.

The student could take the same subject, such as Science, from two different lines. This would reduce the number of subjects he has to sit in the Junior Certificate and double the amount of teaching he is receiving in that subject. This is an extreme solution. Most SLD students are well able to cope taking all the option subjects and in most cases actually enjoy their option subjects far more than their core subjects. Reduction of options may be helpful in the case of students who are severely affected by SLD and are struggling to achieve literacy.

It is difficult to give general advice on what subjects would suit a SLD student as each student has a different profile of abilities. Here are some pointers about subjects which may help in reaching a decision.

Art

Art is a subject without a written exam at Junior Certificate level. At Leaving Certificate level the paper includes written questions on the History of Art. 75% of the final grade in the Junior Certificate is based on projects which the student completes during the exam year. Because the subject is not verbally based, it can provide a rewarding and stimulating subject for SLD students, many of whom have good visual spatial skills. Indicators for success in the subject would be an interest in art and crafts and good hand-eye co-ordination.

Business Studies

Business Studies is one subject at Junior Certificate and splits into the separate subjects of Accounting, Economics and Business at Leaving Certificate. It contributes to the student's understanding of the world of business and encourages a positive attitude to enterprise. The course includes both book-keeping and theoretical content. The book-keeping aspect of the course may be attractive to the SLD students who have good computational skills.

Home Economics

Home Economics is a mixture of practical skills and theoretical content. There is a project and a practical cookery examination during the Junior Certificate year which carry marks towards the final exam. It leads on to the subjects of Home Economics Social and Scientific and Home Economics General at Leaving Certificate. Career possibilities include hotel and catering, food science, fashion, interior design and paramedical careers. Indicators for success in this subject are an interest in the subject matter and good dexterity.

Languages
Should the SLD student take a foreign language? This is a key question for parents. The importance of languages is being stressed as Ireland trades increasingly with her EU partners. Also it is widely believed that students need a third language to attend university. This third language requirement applies only to the colleges of NUI. SLD students can apply for an exemption from this requirement. Details of this exemption are in Appendix E. Some SLD students will never make a success of studying a language and it will become a subject in which they face failure. This can have an effect on how they view school. Indicators that the student should not take a foreign language include difficulty in reading and spelling English, poor achievement in Irish, difficulties remembering the sound of new words and recall of new vocabulary. However the language courses have an increasing oral and aural element, so SLD students with good oral and aural ability may be quite successful in mastering another language. Some schools have an option structure that makes the study of a foreign language obligatory and this may not suit particular dyslexic students.

Materials Technology (wood)
Materials Technology (wood) consists of practical work, theory and drawing. It aims to train students in the use of tools and materials and to develop self-reliance, initiative and accuracy. The Junior Certificate exam consists of a written theory examination and a practical project. It is studied at Leaving Certificate level as Construction Studies and is suited to those interested in careers in construction, architecture and engineering. Indicators for success in the subject are: dexterity, an interest in the subject and a practical approach to problem solving.

Metalwork
Metalwork introduces students to the various processes, tools and materials in modern use. It has a practical and theoretical content. The student can gain experience in interpreting drawings, planning a work sequence and carrying out task. At Leaving Certificate the subject is studied as Engineering and provides a sound and knowledgeable basic

grounding for those interested in engineering or technical careers. Indicators for success in the subject are: dexterity, an interest in how things work and a logical approach to problem solving.

Science

Science is taught as one subject at Junior Certificate level but splits into the separate subjects of Physics, Chemistry and Biology at Leaving Certificate level. It opens the doors to careers in technology, medicine and science. A science subject is a minimum requirement for entry to many third-level courses in these areas. The answers required in the Junior Certificate are factually based with very few essay type answers. This may suit the SLD student. The course includes a large amount of practical laboratory work. Because of the need to be scientifically literate in the modern world, it is advisable for most students to take Science as a subject.

Technical Graphics

In Technical Graphics students are trained in the use of drawing instruments and are given a knowledge of the basic geometrical constructions and their practical applications. This subject leads to the study of Technical Drawing at Leaving Certificate and is suited to those interested in careers in architecture, engineering and other occupations of a technical nature. Indicators for success in the subject are: neatness, good hand-eye co-ordination and a logical approach to problems. Some SLD students excel in visual spatial skills and this subject will suit such students.

The subjects Art, Home Economics, Materials Technology, Metalwork, Science and Technical Graphics have a practical and theoretical content. As a result the student is learning through doing tasks as well as learning the theory content. This multi-sensory approach suits the SLD student.

One subject which a small number of students take is Typewriting. It was taken by less than a thousand students in 1997. It is a skills based subject. Keyboarding skills are highly recommended for SLD students. Typewriting provides a subject in which they might be successful and which would equip them with these essential skills.

IRISH

The student may be exempt from Irish under the Department of Education and Science Directive. Rule 46 of the Rules and Programme for Secondary Schools allows some SLD students such an exemption. One of the grounds for an exemption is that it is given to 'students who function intellectually at average or above average level but have a specific learning difficulty of such a degree of severity that they fail to achieve expected levels of attainment in basic language skills in the mother tongue'. Parents should be aware that this exemption will cover the student for entry to NUI colleges and nursing but not for some careers that have an Irish language requirement, such as teaching. If the student is exempt from Irish, is there any provision for this class time to be used constructively such as remedial withdrawal or computer time?

Is Irish part of the entrance assessment? If it is, does it play a part in deciding class placement? If the student has an exemption or has attended one of the specialised reading schools, such as St. Oliver Plunkett's in Monkstown where the emphasis is on mastery of English, with less emphasis on Irish, is this taken into account in decisions on class placement?

DISCIPLINE

Dyslexics tend to be disorganised. They need an organised classroom with clearly given instructions and a sense of order as they may need to concentrate quite hard to interpret their teacher's instructions. They require a well-structured and disciplined atmosphere in which to learn. Such a classroom provides the teacher with time to ensure the SLD student understands what is expected and allows the teacher to check individual work. It also ensures a pleasant and relaxing environment. In a classroom where the teacher has to impose order constantly, the teacher can be more stressed and have less time to give to individual students. The atmosphere is more tense.

In recent years teachers have observed a greater indiscipline in the classroom. The reasons for this are varied and include: increased amount of family breakdown, less parenting skills so some parents find it difficult to discipline their children and children with little regard for authority who find it difficult to obey discipline imposed by others. The final sanctions open to schools have been reduced. Expulsion of a pupil is extremely rare. Whatever the reasons, there is no doubt the student's progress will be affected if there is difficulty imposing order on a class group.

Students, who are different in any way, can be picked on by bullies. Dyslexic students are different and may become victims of such behaviour. Most schools now have strong anti-bullying policies. It is possible to prepare students to meet bullying behaviour by teaching them coping strategies in advance. Giving them an understanding that such behaviour is a reflection of inadequacies on the part of the bully may prevent them feeling that there is something wrong with themselves which attracts bullying. Make sure that, if a situation arises, they know to talk to the adults in authority.

TRANSITION YEAR

In some schools transition year is part of the curriculum for all students. In others it is not available and in some it is optional. There can be advantages and disadvantages to a transition year for the SLD student.

The advantages of transition year for a SLD student include:

◆ The SLD student may find it difficult to achieve academically. Transition year gives the opportunity to do projects, to obtain new skills, to research possible careers and to experience different methods of working. It is different from the academic work done in the Junior Certificate and the student may do well with this change of approach. Self-esteem may be fragile in the SLD student, who may have had to come to terms with failure in academic areas in the past. Transition year may give him the opportunity to build up self-esteem. Up to now the class may have judged and assessed fellow-students on their academic results. This year will allow other aspects of his personality to show.

◆ It gives time to reflect on the type of CV the student has and how to develop it. Some SLD students will not achieve the academic results to compete for courses where points decide the allocation of places. They may be relying on a good CV to help them at interviews.

◆ Project work will help the SLD student to organise goals, to do research and to meet deadlines. These are skills which many SLD students need to develop. However they may need help and support to do it.

◆ Self-esteem will be enhanced during transition year by
  • Work experience.
  • Learning new skills, such as computer skills, typing and organising projects. If the SLD student does not already use a computer, it is important that he becomes skilled with computers during this year.
  • Contributing to the community. This can be the school community or the wider community. Many transition year programmes include a community element, e.g. fund-raising for charities.
  • Achievements such as the President's Award Scheme (An Gaisce), or sporting exploits all build up self-esteem. The President's Award is

particularly suitable as the student chooses four challenges in each of the following; community work, sport, new skills and an adventurous activity. If the student meets his goals, the award is given.

The disadvantages of a transition year for the SLD student include:

◆ The programme for transition year may be less structured in some schools and students may lose the study skills they have learned and find it hard to return to serious study in fifth year.

◆ The SLD student may already be older than his classmates if he has repeated a year at some stage. Taking transition year may mean he is relatively old sitting the Leaving Certificate.

◆ The SLD student may feel somewhat at sea in the flexible curriculum of transition year. Organising project work and setting goals to achieve long-term objectives may be more difficult for him than for other students.

If the transition year is well planned, it can be of enormous benefit to SLD students. The worry that study skills may be affected because of the lack of a defined programme is offset by the development of skills in handling flexible project-related goals. This adaptability and flexibility needed for such work are skills essential for today's job market and for life.

SIZE OF SCHOOL

Large schools (schools of over 500 pupils) can provide a wider range of subjects. With more choice the SLD student may find subjects that he can do well. Smaller schools will have less subject choice, which can be a disadvantage. On the other hand the smaller school provides an environment where each student is known by all the staff. This can have a beneficial effect on self-esteem and strengthen a feeling of being part of the school community. There may also be smaller classes. There may be less streaming.

CLASS SIZE

It is very much to the SLD student's advantage if class sizes are small. In a small class the teacher has more time to pay individual attention to students. Maximum class size guidelines at second-level are thirty students in academic classes such as English or Maths and twenty-four for practical classes such as Science and Home Economics. In state-funded schools classes tend to be close to these numbers. Some schools try to arrange that the numbers of students in the lowest stream are smaller than in the rest of the classes of the year group. The number of students in classes in private schools can be lower as the private schools have additional funds to employ extra teachers.

SCHOOL ATTITUDE TO SPECIFIC LEARNING DIFFICULTY

Some schools can be very supportive of the needs of SLD students and have structures in place to assist them. However, remember that at second-level, very few teachers have had formal training in what SLD is and how it affects students. Chapter 5 gives details of a survey which shows that the recommended support services are not provided in the majority of Irish schools.

In meeting with the principal of a school for the first time to discuss the needs of the student, it will become apparent whether the school has a supportive attitude or not. This is the time to raise issues such as an exemption from Irish, special consideration in state exams and support services inside the school. Even if the school principal does not accede to requests, the fact that he/she is willing to discuss them will indicate something about his/her attitude.

REMEDIAL FACILITIES

The student, on entrance to second-level, may still need remedial help. Are such facilities available? Will the student benefit from them? The reason for the last question is that there could be a situation where a SLD student is placed in a middle stream class but the remedial facilities in the school are focused on those in the weakest stream or are provided in first year only.

LEVELS OF PAPERS IN THE JUNIOR CERTIFICATE

The Junior Certificate is an examination which replaced the Intermediate Certificate.

In Irish, English and Maths it provides three levels at which the exam may be taken: higher, ordinary and foundation. Roughly about 40% of the students take the higher paper, 50% take the ordinary and 10% take the foundation. The foundation level has been introduced to facilitate students who would have failed to achieve a pass grade in the Intermediate Certificate. Students, who take the foundation or ordinary level in a subject, normally would not go on to sit the Leaving Certificate in that subject at higher level. Foundation Maths at Junior Certificate will lead on to foundation level Maths at Leaving Certificate. *Foundation level Maths and Irish are not acceptable for entry to many courses and careers.* Most regional technical colleges, DIT and WIT courses specify the student must have passed ordinary level Maths as well as ordinary level English or Irish at

Leaving Certificate. The decision that a student drop to foundation level Maths may be taken in second year and can have serious career implications later on.

In all other subjects other than English, Irish and Maths in the Junior Certificate there is a higher level paper and an ordinary level paper. It is intended that the majority of students would take the higher level paper. The ordinary level paper in these subjects is more the equivalent of the foundation level in Irish, English and Maths. A student who wants to do higher level at Leaving Certificate in a particular subject should be taking a higher level paper for his Junior Certificate.

Does the school teach all levels for the Junior Certificate? If ordinary level or foundation level would be more suitable for a particular child, will there be a class at this level? Will the student be in a mixed class with both levels being taught in the same classroom?

TYPES OF STATE EXAMINATIONS

In recent developments of the state examination system, there are now three distinct Leaving Certificates, the traditional exam-based Leaving Certificate Programme, the Leaving Certificate Applied Programme (LCAP) and the Leaving Certificate Vocational Programme (LCVP). These will be discussed in more detail in Chapter Six.

The Elementary Junior Certificate has been introduced in forty-five schools in 1996 for students whose particular needs are not adequately addressed in the broadly based Junior Certificate. It is hoped this programme will reach out to young people who leave school early without obtaining any qualifications. The programme involves greater student activity and specific goals are set for literacy and numeracy. Instead of examination grades, a student profiling system is used to measure achievement. Details of which schools offer this programme are available from the Department of Education and Science.

If parents consider a particular type of state examination programme would suit their child, they should enquire if such a programme is being provided by the school. If the parents are interested in a particular school which does not offer the LCAP or LCVP, they may consider the option of the student changing school after the Junior Certificate or transition year.

CO-ED VERSUS SINGLE SEX SCHOOLS

While there has been research which suggests that girls' achievement in co-ed schools may drop, having worked in a co-ed school for many years, I would have no hesitation in sending a student to either a co-ed or single sex school. However in the case of SLD students, there are some schools where there is a very competitive ethos either academically or on the sporting field. If the SLD student is not achieving academically and is not participating in the major sport of the school, his self-esteem can be affected. In this case I would choose either a school where there is less emphasis on competitive achievement or a co-ed school where, because of the wide mix of students, there are many different types of activities offered.

EXTRA CURRICULAR ACTIVITIES

I have mentioned that self-esteem can be fragile in an SLD student. They have experienced difficulty and failure with the academic part of the curriculum. However they can achieve success and peer recognition in other areas such as the extra-curricular activities organised by the school. Some schools put on a wide range of activities which can include sports of every type, debating, drama, organising a school bank, camera clubs and social concerns such as Amnesty International.

Remember that often it is the student with poor self-esteem who may be reluctant to join in group activities. Parents should become aware of what is available and encourage him to participate.

DISTANCE FROM THE HOME TO SCHOOL

Living close to the school can facilitate students participating in extra-curricular activities. Living at a distance from the school can mean the student misses out on social life and friendships. It is more difficult to participate in many aspects of school life if the student is tied to transport timetables or is relying on parents to provide lifts.

SUMMARY

Several different factors should be considered when choosing a school. There will be no perfect school that will meet all criteria. Parents need to decide on what they consider to be the most important. They should then research the schools in their locality and decide on the school which will meet the student's needs best.

Below is a summary of the points discussed in this chapter. They are not in order of importance.
- ◆ Class placement.
- ◆ Choice of subjects.
- ◆ Irish.

◆ Discipline.
◆ Transition year.
◆ Size of school.
◆ Size of class.
◆ School attitude to SLD.
◆ Remedial facilities.
◆ Levels of papers in the Junior Certificate.
◆ Leaving Certificate and Junior Certificate Programmes provided.
◆ Co-ed versus single sex schools.
◆ Extra-curricular activities.
◆ Distance from home to school.

Coping with Second-Level: How Parents can Help

4

The change to second-level is a big transition for all students. The student is moving from having one teacher all day to having several teachers in the course of a day. There is also the introduction of new subjects. There is more emphasis on exams. The vast majority of students cope well and are very positive about the move and have settled in well by mid-term. However this transition can bring more pressures for the SLD student. The most obvious change is that at primary-level the student will have had one teacher who knows him and his difficulties well. Now the student may face up to nine different teachers in a day. He needs to be organised to face the different demands of these teachers. The primary school curriculum concentrates on numeracy and literacy. Now new subjects appear and must be mastered. It is expected that basic skills in numeracy and literacy are in place. There is a certain curriculum to be covered in time for the state examinations.

Parental interest is a vital component in a student's progress. However there are some extremes to be avoided. Some parents can set unrealistic goals and push the student to achieve these. Others can appear to be disinterested and avoid involvement with schoolwork, perhaps because they themselves found it difficult when they were at school. It must be remembered that dyslexia can be inherited. Others use the student's difficulties as a reason for not making any academic demands at all on the student. However, consistent parental support, based on a realistic knowledge of the student's ability, is invaluable. I believe it to be the most important factor in the development of the dyslexic student's self-esteem and his ability to cope. The parents' role is essential at the start of second-level, but as the student matures, he should gradually take more responsibility for his progress and should apply the appropriate study skills himself. It is a developing process in which the parental input diminishes as the student achieves a growing independence and mastery of the necessary skills.

The reason why parental support is so critical at the start of second-level is that it is important that the SLD student makes a successful transition from primary school. There is a major challenge in coping with all the new subjects and teachers and with the new structure of the school week. If he does not achieve some level of success, there is a risk that, as a defence mechanism, he may turn off the idea of school. Parents can help him meet the challenge of second-level by using some of the more appropriate suggestions below. Certainly not all these suggestions will apply to all students. Read over the list and take the ideas most suitable to your child's particular needs.

HOMEWORK

Homework is very important at second-level. It consolidates learning from the classroom. When material is taught in the classroom, the student hears it for the first time. It is important he understands what he is being taught at this stage. This material which he understands will be forgotten unless the knowledge is consolidated through homework, either written or learning. It will then be forgotten within a few weeks unless it is revised on a regular basis. A revision programme means it will stay in the mind of the student.

Homework can become a battleground, fraught with difficulties. The dyslexic student can be quite tired at the end of a day in school more so than his peers because he must concentrate harder and simple tasks can take him longer to do. Homework may also take him a longer time to complete. If the hours needed to do homework are excessive, talk to the teacher. If it is taking the student an hour to do a question that will be allocated half an hour in an exam, the teacher needs to know this. Long hours spent at homework will only exhaust the student further.

Organisation of homework

Homework should be done as early as possible in the evening, when the student still has energy. At the weekends encourage him to do homework on a Friday night. Some students spend a lot of time 'notting', i.e. spending time not doing the homework while at the same time feeling it hang over them like a cloud. They then feel that homework takes all night because they have been thinking about it all night.

A definite routine will help establish good work practices. Homework should be done at a desk or a table, with the books and any equipment needed near at hand. The student should not study with the television or the radio on. These will interfere with concentration. The student should not be interrupted for telephone calls or callers to the door. An agreement can be made that these calls can be returned after the study time is over.

Many people find it difficult to be organised and tidy but some dyslexics can find lack of order seriously affects their work. A work area with plenty of shelving space; a desk organiser that has a place for pens, staples, paperclips; a filing routine that puts notes into folders every day; the use of different colour folders for different subjects; a routine for clearing out the schoolbag daily and packing it at night for the following day; a study timetable on the wall; these are some ideas that will reduce chaos and muddle. They should use the class timetable to check their bag for the next day. With the lack of order that can characterise their work, they are likely to forget important books and completed homework for different subjects, unless they have a checking system. Is their bag neat, or do scraps of dog-eared paper lurk in its depths? These scraps of paper often turn out to be poems given for learning or vital notes which the teacher has supplied. If they get photocopied pages from teachers, it is essential to use a filing system.

Learning work should also be done at a desk. Some students find pacing up and down helps to improve concentration but the student should never resort to lying down on a bed. It is all too easy to relax and allow the mind to drift off.

Each school will have its own guidelines for homework. I recommend two hours a night for a first year student five nights a week. This will increase in later years. The two hours will include time for written homework, learning homework and revision. It can be helpful if parents and student talk about the demands of homework in the August prior to entry and set out agreed timetables which specify where and when homework is to be done. This can reduce conflict later. Often the scenario is that in October or November, parents can get exasperated with or worried about a student who is doing half an hour of homework and claiming he has no more to do. If parents can refer back to the agreed programme, it will help resolve the conflict. From the student's point of view, he benefits from having clear guidelines on what he should do.

Some SLD students find it very difficult to set goals for homework. Parents should ensure they keep a homework notebook where they write in all the homework they are given, so it can be checked off. It can help if they list all the classes they have in a particular day and write the homework beside the name of the subject. Some teachers write homework on the blackboard, other teachers call it out. Some homework will be written, some will be oral. All should be entered into the homework notebook.

Handwriting and Layout

With written homework, is it the best the student can do or is it carelessly done? If you think it can be improved, try to set higher standards for him. Ask him to proof-read his answers. Reading the work aloud will help identify omissions, grammar, and spelling problems. Some students may not be able to read their own work because of their poor handwriting, so what chance does the poor teacher have? If handwriting is particularly bad, the major problems can include:

◆ The backs of the letters are not straight but go off in all directions.

◆ Letters like 'a, d, g, o, b,' are not closed.

◆ The letters wander above and below the line.

◆ Letters like m,w, u, v, n r, are not clearly formed, so they all look the same.

It can help if the student tries to correct one of these problems at a time. Doing this can greatly improve the readability of the handwriting. Using good quality paper for writing can help as well.

Check on the layout of Maths. Are the columns of figures straight? Often in Maths and Business Studies, mistakes are made because the columns of figures are not aligned or figures are illegible.

All this checking may seem very onerous for parents. It is in the beginning but it is by the consistency of the checking that standards improve. Over time, a routine will become established and the student will adopt many of the practices automatically which means the parents' role will reduce.

Learning Work

Many students consider homework to be the written work given by teachers. The teachers will find out if the written work is not done and there may be punishment work given. However it may be possible to avoid doing some of the learning work given since it can be more difficult for teachers to check that this work is done by all students.

I see learning work as the key to success at second-level. It is the work learnt by students which will be tested in the house and state examinations. The first mistake the student makes is to think learning work is less important than written and to avoid doing it. The next mistake is to think learning or memorising happens by 'reading over' the text several times.

This is a very common error. Reading over a chapter of history twice does not mean that it is learnt and that key points will be remembered. The student needs to think about what he is going to learn and set out a clearly defined goal, e.g., 'I will learn the causes and effects of the French revolution'. He must then use notes or make notes which are learnt off-by-heart.

It may also help at the end of the study period if parents ask a question or two on the topics covered that night. They do not need to understand the material, just open a page and ask a question based on that page. This technique may be helpful to the student by improving the motivation and quality of study because he knows his work will be checked. Also the actual verbal recitation of what he has learned can reinforce the material learnt and help with verbal expression.

Note-taking

Discussion of learning brings up the subject of note-taking. The ability to extract key points is a critical skill at second-level. Good notes make learning the text much easier and also can help in formulating answers as the student has a structure around which he can organise his thinking. SLD students can find note-taking difficult for a number of reasons: poor reading skills, the readability levels of the textbooks, the volume and size of the texts and a lack of ability to summarise.

If they are not good at taking notes, there are books of revision notes for some subjects which are invaluable. These are available in schoolbook shops, both for Leaving Certificate and Junior Certificate levels. At Junior Certificate level, History, Geography, Business Studies and Science are available. For SLD students it can be useful to obtain these notes at the beginning of junior cycle or senior cycle.

When taking notes from a written text, the student should first think about the purpose of the notes and what information he wants to extract from the text. For any student a mass of closely written pages of notes will make revision more difficult than it should be. A mistake many students make is that their notes are far too long. They lift complete chunks of the text and include virtually everything from the main book. Notes should be short, precise, stressing the main points only. Notes should be a third of the length of the text from which they have been taken, preferably even shorter. Layout and presentation of notes can help all students but in particular SLD students, some of whom may be able to hold the graphic image of the notes in their mind and work to recall the content of the notes from this image. Here are some ideas to help make notes clearer:

◆ Leave plenty of space, particularly margins.
◆ Use alternative lines of the page.
◆ Use different colours to highlight names and points to be remembered.
◆ Use headings and sub-headings.
◆ Numbering of relevant points can help their recall.
◆ Use of mind maps to show the interrelationships between facts.
◆ Organise notes, so there is an index at the front and each page is numbered.
◆ Mnemonics can help recall. An example of a mnemonic from my own school days is
FATDAD, for the six counties of Northern Ireland, Fermanagh Antrim, Tyrone, Derry, Armagh, and Down.

Tapes and Videos

Some students will find it useful if their notes are taped. The student is then obtaining the information through the eye and the ear at the same time. It might come down to parents actually taping themselves reading notes or perhaps a group of parents sharing the task of taping. It is of more benefit to tape notes rather than the full textbook as it is the key points the student needs to be able to recall.

Tapes and videos can be useful in teaching the English curriculum. In Junior Certificate English the teacher has a wide choice of material. If the choice of novels include those available on tape, it may be helpful to the student. He can both listen and read at the same time. This will help him recognise words which are unfamiliar. For some SLD students it is so laborious to decipher a page of text that the storyline is lost. Tapes help to overcome this. Ask the teacher to consider choosing texts which are available on tape. In the Leaving Certificate English course, videos and tapes of texts are available. Such aids make the students very familiar with the text, the story and the characters but it does not replace reading the text.

Tapes of novels are a way to widen the student's information and stimulate his imagination. Such students do not read for pleasure. Using tapes of novels gives them access to literature that other students of their age will have read. The library service has many tapes available.

Tapes and videos can also be beneficial in teaching other subjects. SLD students benefit from this multi-sensory teaching. The difficulty is finding tapes and videos relevant to the curriculum of the different subjects. During term time RTE Network 2 have educational programmes on throughout the day. Topics covered include Science, Geography and History.

Spelling

If spelling is a difficulty, the student should keep a spelling notebook in which he writes any new words he meets in each subject and their meaning. The student then learns these spellings by heart. It is often the new words or names that the SLD student can find difficult to recall. The revision of the vocabulary notebook just prior to an exam can aid the recall of these terms.

Some aids to spelling have been developed. Franklin Spellmasters are electronic gadgets similar to a personal organiser. The student can spell a word and it will be checked phonetically and, if incorrect, an alternative spelling is suggested. There is a variety of these aids available, some with a thesaurus and/or a dictionary. Many computers have spell-check programmes.

Essay-writing

Essay writing can pose particular problems for the SLD student. It is a complex task and the student may have difficulty in some or all of the following: understanding the title, organising ideas and thoughts, finding the words to express these thoughts, spelling the words and then punctuation and handwriting. The student can cope better if he takes each of these in turn.

The first thing to do is to read the title of the essay and make sure that it is understood. Pay attention to all the key words in the title. There are certain key words that occur constantly in questions and it is surprising how many students do not know their exact meaning. See Fig. 4.1 for terminology used in questions.

The next stage is to plan the essay. In a narrative type essay which may be given in Junior Cycle, the questions the student should ask himself are Who? Where? When? What? How? Why? and what was the result? This will help him structure his essay in a coherent manner.

In essays where he has to discuss or give opinions, he should take a sheet of paper and develop a mind map of the main outline of the essay, showing ideas he wants to include. This will help in recognising the relationship between different ideas. It will also help to organise the format of the essay. Once this is done, it will be easier to see the structure of the essay and the sequence of ideas. Parents may be able to help here by checking to see that the essay is in logical order and is related to the title of the essay. This will help with paragraphing. Each paragraph should deal with a separate point. The plan should have a clear introduction, development of the topic and a conclusion.

ANALYSE	Break into its component parts, discuss and show interrelations.
ARGUE	Make a case, using appropriate evidence, either for or against the issue.
ASSESS	Consider the value or importance of something, showing positive and negative points and give your point of view.
COMPARE	Identify features that two or more things have in common.
CONTRAST	Identify differences between two or more things.
CRITICISE	Judge the value or truth of a topic, showing your reasons.
DEFINE	Explain something in sufficient detail for it to be distinguishable from similar things.
DESCRIBE	Outline the main aspects of an idea, or show how a thing would appear to the five senses: taste, sight, touch, smell, sound. The five questions (how, why, who, where and when), will provide an mechanism to describe some events.
ENUMERATE	List or number points, possibly using a sentence to describe each.
EVALUATE	Judge the value or importance of something, showing positive and negative aspects.
EXPLAIN	Show how things work, or the sequence in their development. Describing could be part of this.
IDENTIFY	Show clearly the key features of a topic.
ILLUSTRATE	Similar to explain but should be accompanied by relevant drawings, diagrams, etc.
PROVE	Show the truth of a proposition, by presenting evidence to support your argument.
SUMMARISE	Reduce the text down to main points.
TRACE	Show the sequence of events or the interrelationships between topics.

Fig 4.1 Terminology Used In Questions
This list is a guide to the customary meaning of these words.

Having the master plan ready reduces the number of tasks the SLD student now faces. The thinking and structuring has been done, he must find the words to express his ideas. Thinking about what he wants to say and expressing himself aloud may help him find the English he needs. A thesaurus is invaluable in finding the exact word.

Spelling is the next hurdle. It is difficult to suggest a way of handling this. Should the student look up spellings of which he is unsure and interrupt the flow of writing or should spelling be checked at the end and then be corrected? The answer to this depends on what works best for each student. The Spellmaster can help in spelling. Mistakes in punctuation can be picked up if the essay is read out aloud on completion.

It is important that handwriting is at least legible, particularly if the student has to write in examinations and does not have access to computers. If the writing cannot be read, marks will be lost, so it is important to ensure legibility. Perhaps rewriting an essay after the thinking, spelling and punctuation have been completed will produce a more legible end-product. It is, however, very time-consuming.

Essay writing is a key skill not only in English but applies also in answering questions in other subjects. At Leaving Certificate level, essay type answering is required in many subjects such as Business, History, Economics or Geography.

Reading

Reading is a key skill at second-level. Most SLD students will have some reading skills but they will need to pick up on speed and stamina. They often do not like reading. It can be so laborious that the story can get lost in trying to decipher the text. Yet if their reading is to develop, they must practise. It can be difficult to get books to suit the SLD student. Books with a suitable reading level may have a very babyish content. Again the library service has books which may help. Some libraries have adult literacy schemes and have books with adult content, which have been abridged and the vocabulary simplified. These books can be graded for various reading levels. A routine of doing twenty minutes reading daily even throughout the summer can help maintain and develop reading skills.

When reading texts or suggested background reading, the student should read actively. This means he begins by being clear about the purpose of the reading, - what exactly does he want to find out? He should read with a pen in his hand, so he can take note of major points. Making notes will also help with his concentration. The student should check new words in a dictionary.

REVISION

Revision is an important element of work done at home. Written homework, learning homework and revision are the three ways which will help the student achieve. All are necessary. Written and learning homework will be given by the teacher. Both written work and learning by heart will ensure work done in class is understood and consolidate the material covered. However if the student does not revise, he will forget the content relatively quickly. Revision ensures that it is remembered. Part of the student's study timetable should include revision plans. A plan should be made out showing the subjects to be revised after homework each night. An example is given below for a Junior Certificate student.

MONDAY	TUESDAY	WEDNESDAY	THURSDAY	FRIDAY
History	Science	Maths	History	Business Studies
English	Irish	French	Science	Geography
Geography	Maths	Business Studies	English	Irish & French

The student in first year should plan to do two hours work a night. If homework takes an hour the rest of the time would be divided between the subjects for revision. If the student has a lot of homework one night, then the revision could be included in another night's work or the weekend. Adapt it to the student's personal schedule. If he has a scouts' meeting or a sports session one night, leave that night free of revision.

Setting goals is important in revision too. The student should make out a clear target to be learnt in the revision. The important aspect of revision is not the amount of time but the goals which have been met. A student can waste two hours sitting reading over his books. An example of a such a target would be

◆ In Maths, revision of ten theorems and do twenty examples from the textbook based on them.

◆ In Geography, revision of rock types, how to recognise them, where they occur, and what are their uses.

◆ In History, revision of how the monks lived in a medieval monastery, under the headings of work, food, manuscripts and clothes.

Coming closer to exams, revision becomes even more important. About six weeks before the exam, check that the student has the list of topics on which the examination will be based. This could be done on a single sheet of paper with a column for each subject. He may need help from teachers to do this as the dyslexic student can have difficulty in quantifying and organising the work to be done. He then plans to cover a sixth of each subject list per week until the exams start. As he revises a topic he marks it off the list, so that he can see his progress on the chart.

This can also help reduce the anxiety before an exam. The student feels he is in control and he will have completely covered the course before the exam. This feeling of control helps minimise stress and anxiety. Stress is unfortunately part of the educational system. However, for dyslexics, stress and time pressures can make their particular problems worse and their thoughts can jump about and lack order. A clear revision plan, with clear goals, helps in keeping stress levels under control. Other well-known stress management techniques such as healthy eating and regular exercise also help.

The Junior Certificate exam format suits SLD students because in many of the subjects there is a series of brief questions where they are asked to write short answers to demonstrate they know the facts. Handwriting, spelling and composition are less important in this type of answering. There is an enormous jump in the standard of answers needed at Leaving Certificate level. In many subjects at this level the student must be able to construct a longer essay-type answer and show what he knows in his answer. This can pose a challenge to the SLD student who finds longer written answers involving organisation of information difficult.

PROJECT WORK

Projects can cause problems for SLD students. These can include: difficulty in sourcing materials, in picking out relevant points in reading material, in organising the structure of the project and in its presentation. Parents can provide vital assistance in all these tasks. It can give the student a sense of achievement to undertake a project and bring it to completion. When the student is given the project outline, help him work out a time frame for the various parts of it and set a completion date. He is learning valuable skills in organising projects and work as he comes to terms with his time goals. Selecting and narrowing the reading he has to do can help him as well. Computer skills are very valuable in project work as it helps in the organisation, presentation, layout and spelling of the final result. It means that these students can produce a project that looks professional.

COMPUTERS

Computers help SLD students enormously in many different ways including;

◆ Programmes which help identify students who may have a tendency towards dyslexia such as CoPS.

◆ Programmes which develop numeracy and literacy skills. Award Systems has a catalogue of such programmes. These programmes can make learning more fun. Also, as there is a lot of repetitive learning involved in helping a dyslexic achieve these skills, a computer has more patience than a parent or teacher!

◆ Programmes which cover part of the curriculum of some subjects such as Geography, Maths or Biology. Such programmes use a multi-sensory approach which is beneficial to SLD students.

◆ Generally, at second-level and beyond, a computer is invaluable to SLD students. I recommend that these students develop key-boarding skills as soon as possible. Computers mean they are able to present written material of a very high quality. This is particularly useful if their handwriting is poor. It can be very satisfying to see that the results of one's work look really well. Editing and rearranging of text is easy, so students do not have to rewrite laboriously to produce a final copy. Mistakes are easy to correct. The use of a spellcheck will identify some, if not most, spelling errors. There are some mistakes it will not pick up such as the misuse of correctly spelt words. In the Microsoft word processing programme 'Word 7', spelling mistakes are underlined even as the student types which can be useful. There are grammar check programmes as well. The SLD student could also use a programme with a menu of prepared sentences, so when he has to write a letter, he can choose appropriate sentences from that menu. Typing can be quicker than writing and this may be particularly useful in exams. Some colleges allow students to take exams using a computer (see Chapter 9). Seeing his own work on screen can help the student organise his thoughts and can help him proof-read his work. While the computer can help the dyslexic student enormously, he does need good reading skills to take advantage of this help. If the spellcheck produces three alternatives to an incorrectly spelt word, the student must be able to read these to decide which one is correct.

The British Dyslexia Association has booklets available about the use of computers for SLD students. Philomena Ott's book *How to detect and manage Dyslexia* contains an excellent chapter giving practical advice on choosing computer hardware and software. There is a Dyslexia Computer Resource Centre based at the University of Hull which can provide information on new developments in the provision of computer facilities suitable for dyslexics.

The developments in computers have proved to be a boon to dyslexic students. When one looks into the future, there are even more technologies being developed which will minimise the effects of dyslexia. There are programmes being developed including programmes which can scan handwritten text to provide a typed copy, voice-activated computer programmes which make it possible to speak into the computer and get a typed copy, programmes which correct grammar and computers which can read aloud the text. These will certainly remove some of the disadvantages for dyslexic students.

CONTACT WITH THE SCHOOL

Parents should ensure the school has a full profile of the student by sending in a copy of his psychological assessment. It is helpful if they make suggestions based on their experience on what might work best with the student and that these are as specific as possible. Examples of such recommendations could be that notes be photocopied, that the student use revision handbooks or that the student be allowed to produce homework done on a computer. It can strengthen the parents' requests if suggestions such as these are backed by the psychological assessment.

However even if parents have given the psychological report to the school principal, they should not assume that the teachers will be informed of its contents. Schools are large complex organisations and all relevant members of staff may not be informed. The student will have up to ten teachers each year. I suggest making out a sheet explaining the difficulties of the student and any recommendations on what might work best for the student. Parents could arrange to see the teachers individually and give them this sheet. Parents could also send it to the substitute teacher if a teacher is going to absent for a period of time. If reading aloud in class is a major difficulty for the student, teachers need to know this on the first day the student is in the class. Otherwise the student's self esteem and acceptance in the class may be affected.

Parents should check if the student would benefit from an exemption from Irish and ask the school if the student qualifies under the regulations set out by the Department of Education and Science. They should contact the school to discuss whether to apply for special arrangements in the state examinations for their child. This application needs to be submitted through the school eighteen months in advance for both Leaving Certificate and Junior Certificate. If the application for special arrangements is turned down, there is an appeals procedure.

ACLD runs examination preparation classes for SLD students taking the Leaving Certificate and Junior Certificate. These courses can be very useful and are designed to equip the SLD student with the necessary skills. There is a waiting list for places.

OTHER ACTIVITIES

I have mentioned in the first chapter that self-esteem may be low in the SLD student. At second-level he may find subjects for which he has an aptitude and can enjoy. However many subjects still have a high verbal content and the student may be struggling and still experiencing a sense of failure. Self-esteem gives the student the confidence to try out new experiences and to feel he can manage life. A belief in one's self is the key to the transition to an independent adult life. It can be fostered by the student being involved in activities and becoming competent in them. Involvement in sport, obtaining awards such as scouting badges, involvement in community activity such as visiting old people; developing skills such as photography or life-saving; being competent on a musical instrument; getting work experience; these are all activities which can foster self-confidence. Parents can play a role in getting students involved, particularly at an early age. As the student goes through the teenage years, the influence of parents diminishes. It should be remembered that all of these activities contribute to a Curriculum Vitae.

KEEPING GOING

Throughout this chapter I have mentioned ways parents can help the SLD student. These all take time and effort over a long period of time. It can be very fatiguing. It is easy to start the year with good resolution but to keep going consistently through the long months can be tough. It must be remembered that SLD students have to work so hard in comparison to their peers simply to keep up with the class. They often have extra classes. A piece of learning might take them twice as long to do as other students. Writing an essay can be a strenuous exercise for them, whereas for another student it can be a pleasure. They can be tired and frustrated at times. And for all their hard work, they might not get the satisfaction of good grades. Parents also can feel the strain of providing consistent support.

But parents should realise that they can make a contribution to the student's learning and progress that is irreplaceable. No one else can be there everyday on a one-to-one basis. However it is important for parents to realise they are only human and can only do so much. They should pick out the key three or four ways to help that they think most relevant and concentrate on those. I have learnt to do this over the years. My key points were note-taking and goal-setting. There are other suggestions in this chapter which would have benefited the boys but neither they nor I had the energy to pursue them.

The most important contribution parents can make is the development of a loving, secure relationship where the student is prized for himself and not his results and is given a feeling of support and parental backing.

Giving parental support is not a static process. At the beginning parents may be very involved in goal setting, checking homework, setting out revision plans, helping with projects but the intention should be that the student himself would develop these skills and would learn to apply these skills independently. How quickly this happens depends on many variables, such as the student's own abilities, his maturity or his relationship with his parents. It is a process that develops over a number of years. It is important to see the parents' help as a part of this process which will end up with the student taking responsibility and developing his own skills. If such gradual hand-over from parent to student does not take place, the help is a crutch and the student will become dependent on it.

Coping with Second Level: How School Administration and Subject Teachers can Help

5

I have worked as a second-level teacher since 1982 and from my experience I believe that, at this level, there is a lack of knowledge about SLD and a lack of information on effective teaching strategies for SLD students.

This comment does not refer to remedial teachers who have had training and in-service courses on the topic of dyslexia. They have much experience in dealing with the needs of SLD students. Such teachers have extensive knowledge of how to teach literacy and numeracy skills to many students including those affected by dyslexia. Many SLD students have benefited enormously from the invaluable contribution made to their progress by a remedial teacher. I am not a remedial teacher nor am I involved in teaching literacy and numeracy skills. For this reason, I have not included any discussion on the teaching of these skills in this book. I have focused on how school systems can provide support for the SLD student and how subject teachers can help such students to learn.

The fact that many second-level subject teachers are not aware of the needs of such students is not surprising when one considers that there was little or no input on SLD during the teacher training courses in the past. Even now few teachers have done in-service training on the topic.

At second-level the subject being taught takes priority and often the underlying assumption is that every child will successfully absorb information from the teacher in the same way. Consider that at second-level a teacher may teach close to two hundred students in a day. Taking the conservative estimate of an incidence for SLD of 4%, this means that up to eight of those students could be affected by dyslexia. SLD is not like a physical disability where the student can still learn through the normal classroom techniques. It affects the entire dynamic between pupil and teacher. Teaching is about communicating information. Dyslexia affects communication. The teacher may think he/she has effectively given information to the student and this may not be the case. If the teacher is not aware of the symptoms and effects of SLD, the student may be classified as careless, lazy or stubborn. An understanding of dyslexia among the teaching profession will minimise such problems.

In recent years there has been some improvements in the training provided for second level-teachers. The Higher Diploma in Education courses include some information on dyslexia.

There is very little published research information about SLD in Irish second-level schools. In 1996 Robin and Simon entered a project on dyslexia in the Young Scientist Competition. Part of the project was concerned with the incidence of formally diagnosed SLD students in the second-level school population. They also looked at the provision of support services for such students in second-level schools.

A questionnaire was sent to 10% of the second-level schools in the country (seventy-one in total). Fifty schools replied. This gave a response rate of 70%. A total of 24,407 students was covered in the fifty schools. Their conclusions were:

◆ There was an 0.84% incidence of SLD students in the 24,407 students covered by the survey. This is very low in comparison with international statistics, which suggests a 4% to 10% incidence. Dr. B. Hornsby in her book *Overcoming Dyslexia* says, "it is safe to say that recognisable forms and degrees of dyslexia are present in 10% of children in the Western population. ....In only 2% can the dyslexia be considered severe". The British Dyslexia Association estimate that about 10% of children have some degree of dyslexia. This result of 0.84% seems to suggest that there are undiagnosed SLD students in the Irish school population.

◆ A small number of replies indicated that the schools were not aware of what SLD is or how it can affect students. One school said that as all their students went on as far as Leaving Certificate, it did not have any SLD students.

◆ The support services which psychologists recommend for SLD students are not being provided in the majority of the schools surveyed (See Fig. 5.1).

These findings support my conviction that there is an urgent need for:
◆ In-service courses on the topic of SLD for existing teachers
◆ The development of school policy documents on the provision of support for SLD students
◆ More time devoted to the topic on teacher training courses.

Support Service	% of Schools making the Support Service Available (% based on the 50 schools which replied)
Extra time in exams	24%
Questions read to them in exams	28%
Use of school computer in exams	2%
Use of school computer for classwork	4%
Use of school computer for homework	2%
Use of own computer in exams	0%
Use of own computer for classwork	10%
Use of own computer for homework	12%
Use of a tape recorder in exams	30%
Photocopies of teachers' notes	34%
Choosing texts which are available on tape	34%
Allocating a teacher with special responsibility for SLD students	62%
Study skills training for SLD students	26%
Screening procedures at entrance to second-level	54%

Fig 5.1 Support services provided in Irish second-level schools.

HOW SCHOOL ADMINISTRATION CAN HELP THE SLD STUDENT

Below are ideas on how the school administration and school structures can help the SLD student.

Exemption from Irish

Irish is a compulsory subject and all students in Ireland have to study it as far as Leaving Certificate. Rule 46 of the Rules and Programme for Secondary Schools allows some students an exemption from Irish. It is given to 'students who function intellectually at average or above average level but have a specific learning difficulty of such a degree of severity that they fail to achieve expected levels of attainment in basic language skills in the mother tongue'. In most schools an alternative subject to Irish is rarely provided. This means the student has one less subject in state examinations and also has extra free time. If the school could provide something constructive to do in this time such as giving the student English reading, remedial tuition or extra computer time, it would be a positive use of the free time.

Special arrangements in State Examinations

The SLD student can apply through the school for special arrangements in the taking of state examinations. This application must be made about eighteen months prior to the examination. The school sends the application to the Department of Education and Science and usually includes a psychological report and samples of the student's work. If an application for special arrangements is turned down by the Department of Education and Science, there is an appeals procedure.

There are various forms of special arrangement. The most common is that the examiner is informed of the student's difficulties. The letter from the Department of Education states:

♦ The examiners to whom the above named candidate's scripts will be assigned for correction will be informed of the school's concern regarding the readability of his/her work and will be instructed, if they have difficulty in reading the scripts, to send them to an examiner who is more experienced in marking work which is difficult to read because of mis-spellings, bad handwriting, poor grammar, etc. Every possible effort will be made to mark the candidate's work reliably in accordance with the marking scheme and to ensure that he/she is given full credit for all the work done.

Where the degree of impairment is severe, further arrangements may be deemed appropriate. A candidate who is unable to read, or is effectively unable to read, may be allowed the service of a person who will read the questions. A candidate who is unable to write, or is effectively unable to write, may be allowed the service of a scribe or the use of a mechanical aid such as a tape recorder, a typewriter or a word processor.

Teachers and parents should consider what would be the appropriate type of arrangement for a particular student. Here is an example which illustrates this point.

A student entered second-level who had been diagnosed as SLD and had attended St. Oliver Plunkett's School in Monkstown. He had received remedial help and had good family support. He was co-operative and pleasant and always did his homework. At Christmas he took History as one of his first exams. He got 8%. The teacher was unhappy to give him such a poor mark. He had worked hard during the term and had seem to understand what was being taught. She was worried that his self-confidence would be badly affected by such a low mark. It was decided to read the exam paper to him and write down his answers. His marks went from 8% to 55%. He had got similarly poor marks in Geography and Science. His teachers gave the tests orally and his grades in Science went from 12% to 54%. In Geography his grades went from 11% to 44%. If the history teacher had not raised the issue of his grade, he would have failed his Christmas tests badly. As it was, he did quite well. Also the school would not have become aware of the huge discrepancy between his written and oral performances. Below are examples of his answers on the written test and his answers from the oral test.

Geography short questions	His written answer	His answer after the question was read to him and his answer written down
Magma is	volcanic metel	molten material inside the earth core
Three things that happen at the plate margins are	earthqua volceno	earthquakes volcanoes geysers
The three rock types are	ignus metamorphic	metamorphic igneous sedimentary
Three uses of limestone are		making churches making fireplaces
A slag heap is		dust from a coal mine
Weathering is		rain falls on rock, and wears the rock away
A permeable rock is a rock which		water gets through

His lack of ability to read accurately and quickly and to express his knowledge in written form are major impediments to his passing written exams, yet he has the knowledge if he is examined orally. In his case the school requested a reader and the facility to tape his answers in state examinations.

Communication among the staff

In another incident this student also provided an example of how important it is that all relevant school staff be informed of a student's difficulty. The student had a detention. The Year Head, who was supervising the detention, was not aware of his learning difficulties and handed out the usual assigned work. The student was not able to do it. At the end of the detention period he was given another detention because he had not done the required work. It was sorted out later but he was very upset, as was the Year Head when informed of his reasons for not completing the assignment.

A communications system should be set up which will routinely inform the staff of a particular student's difficulties at regular intervals.

Special arrangements in house and mock examinations

If the student's difficulties are such that he is getting special arrangements in state exams, it is only fair that such consideration also be given in the house exams. This should be part of school policy on SLD. Teachers should be reminded of the student's difficulties prior to the exams and, if appropriate, arrangements made for him to take the exams orally or to have papers read to him.

If sending mock papers outside the school for correction, a note should be attached to the paper explaining the student is receiving special arrangements in the state exams. An incident which illustrates the importance of such communication is the case of a SLD student who sat a Junior Certificate honours English mock paper. The paper was returned with the comment that the spelling was so disgraceful that honours level English was out of the question. This had a negative effect on his confidence when sitting the actual exam in the Junior Certificate where he did have special arrangements which made allowance for mis-spellings.

Correcting exam papers for SLD students will take more time. Poor handwriting, bizarre spellings and poorly expressed facts can mean the teacher has to decipher the script to see if the student has the correct answers. One example of this is where a student lost six marks in a Science exam for saying that a bimetallic strip 'would bend' under heat. However he spelt 'bend' with six letters (bouend) and it was marked as an incorrect answer. Other examples of mispellings from SLD students are: amjedidly for immediately, yooniform for uniform, anctus for anxious, enchivative for initiative and raleigh for rally. These words look totally wrong but they are close enough phonetically for the word to be recognised if the examiner says them aloud.

If the Department of Education and Science allows a student to sit his state exams by using a tape recorder to record his answers, he will need training in this technique. He should also be allowed to tape his answers in his house exams.

Photocopying notes and use of revision books

All students can benefit greatly from good notes. My preference is that a student summarise his textbooks himself as it helps him absorb the information. However it is likely that SLD students will find it very difficult to summarise material in books and make their own notes. This can be due to poor or slow reading where they may have to reread a piece several times to see the points the writer is making, difficulties in summarising and organising material or difficulties in the presentation of legible and clearly laid-out notes.

They can benefit hugely from getting precise and concise notes, either from developing their own skill in note-taking or getting copies of the notes of others. Good notes give them the means to learn. Some SLD students have difficulty seeing and organising patterns. Good notes are an effective way for them to see the structure of what they are learning. The notes are a useful device in organising material and a help in formatting their own answers. Some of the revision handbooks are of use if the student is not provided with photocopied notes. I recommend, in the case of SLD students, they use them from the beginning of first year when they start the Junior Certificate courses and from the start of fifth year for the Leaving Certificate.

If teachers dictate their own notes to the class, it can be problematic for SLD students. If necessary, the teacher should arrange for photocopies of notes to be given to the SLD student. These could be photocopies of the teacher's own notes or a photocopy of the notes of a student who takes well-organised, legible notes. If the teacher calls out notes, some SLD students have a difficulty in visualising the words being called. They have to think about the shape of the words and then they have lost the next point the teacher makes. Here is an excerpt from an essay a sixteen year old girl wrote about her dyslexia.

◆ My head ached, letters churned in my mind. I wanted to scream. I glanced at my friend's masterpiece, every word spelt correctly and a page of beautiful writing, the work teachers love. Slowly I looked at my own copy, half finished sentences, words spelt incorrectly. I placed my hand over my work, embarrassed in case any one would see it. As the Junior Certificate approached and more notes were being called out, the more lost I became. Each time a letter was spelt out to me, it became more jumbled. I got so frustrated. I wanted to give up. I would go out with my friends, when deep down I knew I should be studying. But there seemed little point. I would study and make notes, but I seemed to remember very little. I know that something was wrong, but did not know what. Finally it dawned on me. Maybe I had a learning problem. I could not explain but I had a funny feeling it was dyslexia. I did not know much about it. My parents were very supportive. I was diagnosed in July as having dyslexia. In a way I felt relieved to know I had dyslexia and that I was not thick. I felt angry and confused and wished I did not have it What angered me most was finding out two weeks before my Junior Certificate, as I worried I would not be able to spell words in the exam.

She was a student who had gone through primary school without being identified as SLD. When she did her entrance test, her scores were in the average range. There were no perceived weaknesses on her profile of ability. During her first three years in the school she worked very hard but was always disappointed at her results. She felt it took her much longer than others to absorb written material. She had to reread articles many times to make sense of them. She was spending longer hours on homework than the school would recommend. In May, prior to her Junior Certificate, the frustration of trying to take notes overwhelmed her. She could not visualise what she was to write when the teacher called out notes. She had developed coping mechanisms such as copying from a friend or waiting for others to ask the teacher to repeat a phrase. If the teacher spelt something out, she virtually had to translate the spelling into what the word looked like. If the teacher said 'double O', she would have to ask herself what does that look like. She spoke to her parents saying that she thought she was dyslexic. She went for testing and was diagnosed as having a specific learning difficulty. Because she had worked hard and had learnt to read at the expected ages, she had gone undiagnosed until this stage.

Have a look at the notes in Fig. 5.2 and ask which notes could you learn from best?

(A)
Implications of the Companies Act 1980

1. If a company has engaged in reckless trading, a director may become a restricted director. He may not be able to take part in a company for five years and lose limited liability.

2. A director involved in fraud or dishonesty may be disqualified for a stipulated period.

(B)

(C)
emplications of the companies act 1980

1. If the company has begoy in recless trading, a director may become a restricted director he may not be able to take part in a company for 5 year and loes limited liability

2. A director involve in frude or disonesty may be disqualified for a stipputated period.

Fig. 5.2   (A) shows typewritten Business Organisation Notes which were dictated.
(B) shows the notes taken by a dyslexic student
(C) shows the typed written version of the student's notes

A school policy that would allow the photocopying of notes is of benefit to SLD students.

Tapes

Tapes of notes or texts can help some SLD students learn. The material is being presented to two senses, sight and hearing. Teachers could suggest to parents or to the student himself that notes be taped, in order to see if this is beneficial.

In some subjects, in particular English, videos and tapes of texts are commercially available. If reading is very laboured, the student can lose the thread of the story because it is such hard work to decipher the text. Listening to a tape of a novel while he reads it can mean he can become engrossed in the story. He does not have to look up difficult words as he hears them. He can get familiar with characters and plots. If the poems he has to learn are taped, it can help him to become familiar with them. Videos of Shakespearean plays make the play come alive and make it easier to write about. It does not replace reading the play which needs to be done for the student's own reading development and to make him familiar with the spelling of names, but it helps his knowledge of the text.

In Junior Certificate English, the teacher has great freedom to choose texts. It makes sense that if there is a SLD student in the class that the teacher would choose textbooks which are available on tape.

If the student is not a reader, the teacher could encourage him to widen his knowledge of literature by using tapes. For some SLD students reading does not become any easier. They may have good functional reading skills but reading will never become a pleasurable activity. Part of their coping mechanism is to look for alternative ways to get information and be up-to-date with current books. Tapes, radio and television can provide other routes to information.

Screening and identification of SLD pupils

Up to 1996 there has been no screening test for dyslexia, either at primary school level or at second-level. Psychological assessment was suggested by teachers if the child failed to achieve in reading and writing by the age of eight or nine. So, while it is likely that severely affected SLD students would be identified, border-line cases who achieved reading could slip through the net. Dr. B. Hornsby in her book *Overcoming Dyslexia* calls these students 'hidden dyslexics' and suggests it is only when their earlier promise is not fulfilled in exams that teachers and parents begin to ask questions.

Since 1994, ten students have been diagnosed as having SLD in my own school. All ten had gone through primary school without being identified as having a learning difficulty. Two students were identified from the Differential Aptitude Testing done in third year and went for assessment. One of these students had a percentile score of seventy-five in abstract reasoning and two in verbal reasoning. One student, out of frustration, had raised the question herself because of her difficulties in taking notes down. Another student was identified from the entrance assessment which showed top ability across the board except for spelling which was significantly below average.

I believe that there are many students going through the education system in Ireland who have not been diagnosed and who are frustrated and confused by the demands made upon them.

New screening tests became available in 1996 (See Chapter 2). Particularly important are the tests for the younger age group. It is important that students with SLD are identified in their early years at primary level before they start to fail and their self-esteem suffers.

The DST (Dyslexia Screening Test) is now available to help screen students in the age-group 6 years and 6 months to 16 years and 5 months. This test should be made available in all second-level schools. It could be used if a teacher has any suspicion that a student may have dyslexia. It is important that teachers be aware of inconsistencies and behaviour that might indicate SLD. These could include:

◆ Bizarre spelling, e.g. emplocashuns for implications.
◆ Phonetic spelling of common words, e.g. barax for barracks.
◆ Omission of the endings of words, e.g. essa for essay.
◆ Confusion about the shape of letters such as b and d.
◆ An uneven profile of ability, e.g. very good maths but very poor verbal skills.
◆ A mismatch between verbal performance and written performance.
◆ A difference between verbal and abstract reasoning. It may be noticeable on the AH2 or AH4 test or on the Differential Aptitude Tests (DATS).
◆ Confusion about left and right, or direction.
◆ Transposition of parts of words or letters inside a word or in a sequence of numbers.
◆ Frequent loss of place when copying from the board or reading from a page.
◆ Confusion about simple sequences such as the months of the year.
◆ A slow rate of work, yet good results if ample time is given.
◆ Difficulty in recognising rhyme, such as star, far, jar.
◆ Badly formed handwriting.
◆ Difficulty in following a sequence of instructions.

A combination of several of these indicators should lead teachers to question whether there is a specific learning difficulty present. The teacher should then consult with the student's parents. It is only with a psychological assessment that a diagnosis of Specific Learning Difficulty can be made. The psychological assessment may be done by the Department of Education Psychological Service or by the Health Boards'

Psychological Service but unfortunately there are long waiting lists. Understaffing of the School Psychological Service means the majority of Irish school children have limited access to a psychological service. In 1996 there were thirty-seven psychologists working in the service. A report on the service produced in that year by IMPACT, the union which represents the Department of Education psychologists, suggested that two hundred and fifteen psychologists are needed to provide an adequately staffed service. Due to long delays in getting appointments, many parents opt for a private assessment. The assessment takes two to three hours. It can cost well over a hundred pounds.

Extra Curricular Activities

Most writers on dyslexia describe the effect SLD has on self-esteem and confidence. The student has experienced failure from a very early age in a key part of life, that of academic achievement. It is also a very public arena since all students in a classroom know the student who has difficulties in achieving. This failure in academic achievement can ripple into many aspects of life affecting relationships with peers, engendering a lack of confidence which may lead him into not trusting his abilities and being unwilling to try or join in new experiences. These problems can be worse if the SLD is not diagnosed until second-level.

Some SLD students may find an escape mechanism from being thought 'stupid and thick' by avoiding school work and by confronting authority. It is more acceptable among the student's peers that poor grades are the result of being a 'tough' man rather than the result of a learning difficulty. Others have become expert in evading work. Since many teachers have not been trained to recognise and deal with SLD, these students can get away with these avoidance tactics. This highlights the need for teacher training.

As part of school policy, some brief description of SLD and how it affects students should be given perhaps in the pastoral care programme or the study skills programme. It makes it easier for the SLD student to be open about his difficulties when other students understand what dyslexia is. He may also realise that other students can also be affected and that he is not alone.

SLD students are likely to experience failure to some extent in their academic studies. If self-esteem and confidence are to be developed it will be in other aspects of life. It is really important that these students get involved in activities where they can achieve and be part of the wider school community. Sometimes, because of their low self-esteem, they will be reluctant to join in extra-curricular activities and may need active encouragement from parents and school staff. Types of activities may include all types of sports, clubs, drama, voluntary work and projects. Part of the support service the school should offer is active intervention in encouraging these students to become involved in such activities.

School Structures

Below are some points which might be considered when a school is looking at the support services it provides for SLD students.

◆ If the student has exceptionally weak reading and writing skills, is there an assessment to check if there is a significant difference in his exam performance if he takes an exam orally with a reader and with a taping facility? This would be to ascertain if it would be appropriate to apply for such facilities in State exams.

◆ If there is streaming, does it take account of the SLD student who may be very intelligent and articulate but who has some verbal difficulties?

◆ Is placing such a student in a lower stream class the best option?

◆ If places in a particular option are limited, would the school consider giving positive discrimination to such students when allocating places?

◆ If a student has excellent Maths but poor language skills, will the student have the option to do Honours Maths?

◆ If the student's verbal skills are so poor that he might have difficulty understanding the format of questions in the entrance assessment, does the school make a reader or other assistance available to him? Whereas a reading test will give an accurate picture of his reading skills, a Maths test, where the student does not understand what he is being asked because of the language content or sequencing of the questions, does not measure his Maths ability.

◆ If Irish is part of the entrance assessment and the student has an exemption from Irish, is there a mechanism to take this into account in the overall placement?

◆ If the student is exempt from Irish, is it possible to arrange for another subject or activity to be done during this free time?

◆ Is a third language obligatory in the option structure?

◆ Is remedial tuition available in first year? In later years? Is it available if the student is not in the weakest classes?

◆ Does the student have access to computers? Can extra computer time be made available so the student can develop good keyboard skills? If

this cannot be done in school time, can it be arranged after school? Parents may be willing to pay for this.
◆ Has the staff received in-service training on SLD?
◆ Are the staff reminded on a regular basis of the needs of these students?
The answers to these questions will often depend on school resources.

School Policy

Does the school have a policy document on meeting the needs of SLD students? As the publishing of school plans becomes more widespread, this policy should be part of such a plan. It could provide for the following:
◆ The provision of a staff member who would be responsible for such students.
◆ A statement on the provision of support services the school would provide to help the student achieve his potential, e.g. photocopies of notes, acceptance of computer generated homework and the maximum possible use of tapes.
◆ A statement on the provision of support services during house exams, which would be similar to those provided at the state exams.
◆ The provision of information to the staff on dyslexia.
◆ Regular reminders to the staff about the students affected.
◆ The provision of a screening programme.
Ireland falls far behind the U.K. in providing such a policy. In the U.K. the Education (Special Educational Needs) Regulations 1994 state that governing bodies of schools must draw up a policy document for children with special educational needs (SEN) and that they must report annually to parents on its implementation.

Some of the topics included in a policy document on SEN are:
◆ The objectives of the policy.
◆ The name of the teacher appointed as a SEN co-ordinator.
◆ Arrangements for co-ordinating educational facilities.
◆ Special facilities provided for such pupils.
◆ An identification and assessment programme.
◆ Evaluation and monitoring of the programme.
◆ Liaison with outside bodies.
◆ Details of the in-service training provided.
A future development in Ireland could be that schools might give a teacher the responsibility for implementing the school's policy for SLD students, a role similar to the SEN co-ordinator in the U.K. One of the posts of responsibility in the school could be allocated to such a position.

How Subject Teachers can Help the SLD Student

Some of the topics in the previous section would be relevant to the subject teacher such as note-taking and taping. However there are specific techniques which the subject teacher can use in the classroom which will help the SLD student.

I appreciate how difficult some of them may be to implement for a busy class teacher. At second-level a teacher might easily deal with two hundred students in a single day and have classroom contact with a particular class for only three hours in that week. To tailor teaching techniques to meet individual needs takes time and time is at a premium. However some of these students will fail unless teachers are aware of their specific difficulties and try to find some teaching methods which will help them to achieve. Below are ideas which may help:

◆ Break down a series of instructions into simple commands. Do not give an instruction which is a complicated sequence, e.g. 'After you have taken down your homework and before you leave the room, clean the desk'. Break it down to a series of simpler commands, 'take down your homework', 'clean your desk', 'now you can leave'. The student, who has difficulty with sequences or who has to decipher what is being said, gets confused unless instructions are kept simple.

◆ Some SLD students have difficulty remembering sequences such as days of the week or months of the year and this can lead to conflict with adult demands. A student may have been given homework as follows: an essay for Monday, Maths for Tuesday, revision of a text in Geography for next Thursday, reading for a book report to be handed up in two weeks time. Teachers assume he sees time and sequence clearly in much the same way as they do. However, because of sequencing difficulties, he may confuse the instructions. He then gets into trouble with teachers for not having his work done. It is easy for adults to conclude that he is lazy or careless. Ensure he uses a homework notebook properly with a system that will remind him of tasks.

◆ Give written notices of events. Most second-level students are more than capable of listening and taking home clear details. However it is very possible that SLD students will neglect to take home a key fact or give jumbled information.

◆ Some students will understand the sequence of steps in a Maths problem, a Science experiment or a book-keeping problem in class and appear to be competent but they become confused over the sequence later. Whereas the average student might need to do an example four or five times to be sure of the sequence of steps, the SLD student may need to overlearn the sequence by doing more examples.

◆ Some students may not recognise what it is they are being asked to do in a question. It is important that they are taught how questions are structured and what are the precise meanings of words used in questions. The small link words may be overlooked and yet these radically affect the meaning of a question.

◆ Check if the pupil is willing to read aloud. Some would prefer to do so and not be treated differently from the rest of the class. Others are very conscious that their reading skills are laboured and this anxiety can make their reading worse.

◆ When reading textbooks, introduce the content, so the student becomes tuned in to the gist of the material and keywords. This will help with comprehension. If it is a text with questions at the end of sections, get the student to read the questions before reading the text, so he knows what points are relevant.

◆ Be understanding when giving poetry or other sequences to be learnt off-by-heart. Some SLD students find it exceptionally difficult to remember a sequence regardless of how much time they spend on it. Some SLD students do not register rhyme as a pattern. In learning poetry, if a verse had line endings such as: hood, good, wood, they were as likely to say forest for wood. They have understood the poem and know the ideas and content but they do not perceive the rhyming pattern.

◆ If the student has difficulty in structuring what he wants to say, arrange to give extra time so he can get his thoughts together. The same applies when asking a question. Remember some SLD students have to decipher the question and then formulate their answer. This can put them under time pressure and adds to their anxieties and frustration in the class. They can spend a lot of time worrying about being asked questions. Under pressure they can resort to wild guesses. One technique which would help is if the teacher arranges with them (privately) that they will be asked questions only when the teacher is standing in a particular place. This will mean they can relax for the rest of the time and concentrate on what is being said. Another technique when asking them a question is for the teacher to ask the question, turn and write something on the board and then look for an answer. The student has had time to put his thoughts together.

◆ Some SLD students have difficulty recalling the name of an object or person. A student could know all about Leonardo Da Vinci and yet have difficulty recalling his name. He might guess wildly or else pepper his description of Leonardo's work and times with 'you know your man'. Such students should overlearn the names of people and objects. One method of doing this is to use vocabulary notebooks which contain new words and names in each subject. These can form the basis for revision just before an exam as it is these words that are most likely to have been forgotten.

◆ This next point is one that applies to me personally. I get totally mixed up about right and left. When being taught anything to do with motor skills, such as gym, using a computer mouse or learning to drive, I have to interpret and decipher what the instructor says. If the gym instructor says 'do this', and does a particular action, I have to break it down, analyse what he has done and work out how I have to move to copy it. Once I have learnt how to do an action, it becomes automatic. This illustrates the point that students who may not have academic difficulties can still be affected in other subjects such as Physical Education, Home Economics, Technical Graphics, Science or Art. They have to interpret what is being said and then work out how to do it. It is as though they have to translate the instruction. This can make them appear slow and lacking in concentration.

◆ When correcting, be sparing in the use of red pen. Not all mistakes need to be marked. Take a particular category of error and correct it. There is a greater chance that the student will learn from this. A comment such 'improve your writing' will have little effect on the standard of writing. The student may not know how to improve his handwriting. Try to identify one fault which he can work on such as 'closing the loops in letters such as a, d, g'. Remember it will have taken the student longer than his classmates to produce this homework and it is disheartening if it is full of corrections. If the student has difficulty handing up nicely presented work, get him to use copies with fewer pages, so he has a fresh start more frequently. If the idea is right, give marks regardless of spelling, layout and presentation. Take time to check out bizarre spellings. Since self-esteem can be low, positive encouragement is needed, which is why it is so important that the student gets credit for work done. However for self-esteem to be fostered, the achievement of the pupil must be real. The student will be aware if praise is given for poor work and he could become cynical. This may mean he may not believe praise given to worthwhile work.

◆ Order and structure may need to be taught to some SLD students whereas most students at second-level have learnt how to lay out their work and organise their studies. Some ideas here would be to use Maths copies with squared paper to help keep figures in columns or take the student aside and show him how you want a page laid out. Write out an example to which the student can refer.

◆ Give him a structure for attempting longer written answers. Show him the question, break it down into its constituent parts. Too often his answers will be too short because he does not develop a structure. He feels if he thinks of one point, it is sufficient, instead of attempting to show all he knows about a topic. Mind maps are a very useful technique here. Show him how to sketch out his answer and the points he wants to include before he starts to write his answer. Often the questions: How? Why? Where? When? Who? and What happened? will provide a basic structure for the student to fill in the information he knows.

◆ If spelling is a problem, the student should use a vocabulary notebook in each subject. When the student comes across a new word, he should enter it into the notebook. Encourage the student to learn the spellings in this notebook. Use of multi-sensory teaching of spellings will help retention. This could involve the following steps
  • The student looks at the word picking out any difficult parts of the word.
  • He says the spelling.
  • He traces the spelling. If the student is asked to write the spelling out ten times, very often he will begin to spell the work incorrectly. Tracing means the word remains correct.
  • The student now writes the spelling from memory.
  • He checks if it is correct.
  • He then uses the word in a sentence.

◆ Encourage the student to use computers. Accept homework done in this format, as long as it is filed in an organised way. Computers can liberate the SLD student. The only drawback to this is the fact that the student might not have the use of a computer in the state exams.

◆ Because a SLD student can tend to be disorganised and lack structure in his work, he needs very clear guidelines and revision plans. Before an exam, write out the material which will be examined, so he has a precise agenda. The clearer this is, the better. Allocate sections of work to particular weeks. Within a chapter, give the major headings for revision. These students benefit enormously from study skills workshops.

♦ Multi-sensory teaching can help learning. If lessons include written, oral and visual elements, these provide more 'hooks' for the student to remember the content.

♦ Write clearly on the board. Give him time to take down the information. A SLD student may find this task difficult. Owing to poor memory skills, he may forget what he has to write down and then will not be able to find the place easily when he looks up at the board.

♦ Make sure the student has a 'picture' of the course being covered. When introducing new work, give an overview of the topic. It can help the student see the structure and can draw the different strands together for him.

♦ Check the readability of texts. Peer, in an article in the British Dyslexia Association Newsletter in 1996, described the Fogg Index which can be used to calculate the readability of texts. It can be calculated by looking at the average number of words in a sentence and the number of words with three syllables or more.

♦ Listen to what parents say about the student. Take into consideration their views on which teaching methods are successful. They have had the closest contact with the student and also may have to participate more often in homework than the parents of non-SLD students.

♦ Look for suggestions in the psychological assessment on what teaching strategies may work with the particular student.

♦ Besides listening to the student, parents and the psychologist about the most appropriate and successful approaches to learning and exams, the teacher also needs to develop his/her own ideas on what will work with the student.

CONCLUSION

It is time for second-level schools and teachers to be more aware of the needs of SLD students and develop support systems to meet these needs. Many of the support services mentioned above are already being provided in third-level colleges. However, if there is to be a growth in teacher awareness, in-service training courses for existing teachers must be provided as well as adequate input on teacher training courses.

It cannot be denied that trying to meet the needs of a SLD student in the classroom will place enormous demands on the teacher who will need empathy, patience, extra time and imagination to present the courses in different ways and many teachers are already stressed with the demands made upon them.

In justice, SLD students deserve that the school system is supportive of their needs and that their teachers, if they find the students cannot learn the way they normally teach, look for different methodologies to teach them the way they can learn. Subject teachers, who must meet the demands of the state exam system, realistically may find it difficult to give enough individual attention to one particular student who experiences learning difficulties. On the other hand, a teacher, who has an understanding of dyslexia and adapts teaching strategies as much as possible, will do much for such students.

There is also a reward for the teacher when these students do achieve. Dyslexics can be enthusiastic learners when they find techniques that work for them. Since they are of average or above-average intelligence and have only been held back by their verbal difficulties, they can make very good progress, which is hugely satisfying for the students, their parents and their teachers. With increasing confidence and new learning strategies, SLD students can confound earlier predictions about their achievement.

Options after Junior Certificate

6

The Report on the Economic Status of School-leavers published by the ESRI in December 1997 shows a rapid decline in the proportion of students leaving school after Junior Certificate. A third of all students had left school after Junior (Intermediate) Certificate in 1980. By 1996 this had dropped to 15%.

Unemployment rates are dramatically higher amongst those who leave school early or without qualifications. The rates are below:

Category	Unemployment rate
School-leavers with no qualifications	61%
School-leavers with Junior Certificate	25 – 29%
School-leavers with Leaving Certificate	7 – 10%

The Report also shows how rates of pay are directly correlated with qualifications:

Category	Average Hourly rate
School-leavers with no qualifications	£2.55
School-leavers with Junior Certificate	£2.87
School-leavers with Leaving Certificate	£3.52

The ESRI report shows an improvement in employment prospects for school-leavers in recent years. In 1994 34% of school-leavers were employed one year after leaving school. In 1996 this figure had risen to 44%. The one group which did not appear to benefit from the improved employment prospects is school-leavers with no qualifications. The unemployment rate for this group has remained at approximately 61%. These facts make a very strong case for students to stay on in education.

I would never advise students to leave school after their Junior Certificate unless they have plans that will further their qualifications and skills. It need not necessarily be a traditional Leaving Certificate. Options available include:

◆ Apprenticeships.
◆ Youthreach.
◆ Employment.
◆ National Training and Development Institute Courses.
◆ Leaving Certificate Traditional.
◆ Leaving Certificate Applied.
◆ Leaving Certificate Vocational.

APPRENTICESHIPS

Apprenticeship is the route to becoming a skilled craftsperson. The apprentice works for an employer in a chosen occupation and learns the necessary skills and knowledge. Apprenticeships are standard-based. This means the apprentice will have specific tests and assessments to ensure he meets certain pre-set standards of competency and skill. Apprenticeships comprise on-the-job training with the employer and off-the-job training in a FAS training centre or in an educational college.

The entry requirements for apprenticeships are that the applicant has reached 16 years of age and has obtained a D grade in five subjects at Junior Certificate level. Although Junior Certificate is the minimum requirement for entry, most apprentices actually have a Leaving Certificate.

There are very few apprenticeship places available. In 1994 there were 7,500 applicants for 100 apprenticeship places in the ESB (Electricity Supply Board). This shows what the competition for apprenticeship places is like. There are three routes to an apprenticeship place:

◆ Some apprenticeships, such as the ESB, Aer Lingus, the Army and Aircorps, will be advertised in the national papers. If the apprenticeship is advertised in the national papers, the number of applicants rises. Apprenticeship places in state employment are normally advertised.

◆ Register with the local FAS office who may know of employers looking for apprenticeships.

◆ Apply directly to local firms. The FAS office and the Golden Pages may help when compiling a list of firms.

If a student is offered an apprenticeship, it is important to check that it is a fully recognised apprenticeship, that the student will achieve certification at the end of the period and the firm will release him for off-the-job training. Within two weeks of starting an apprenticeship, the apprentice should register with FAS. FAS actively encourages girls to apply for apprenticeship places including offering a bursary to employers.

RACE, Curragh House, Kildare, offers apprenticeship training for jockeys.

YOUTHREACH

Young people who leave school without any qualification or with a Junior Certificate only are the most vulnerable in the job market. Statistics show the highest unemployment and lowest wages are amongst this group. Youthreach is a special programme sponsored by the Department of Education and Science and the Department of Enterprise, Trade and Employment to give early school-leavers a second chance.

Youthreach seeks to prepare and help these young people to get their first job which will lead to greater long-term employment. Youthreach is available in over ninety FAS and VEC funded centres. The training and work experience lasts two years for those with no educational qualification and nineteen months for those with a Junior Certificate. Trainees receive regular FAS allowances and a certificate on successfully completing the course.

EMPLOYMENT

While there is more employment available in recent years for students with no qualifications or with only their Junior Certificate, the work is mostly low wage employment, much of it part-time or temporary, with poor prospects of training or promotion.

NATIONAL TRAINING AND DEVELOPMENT INSTITUTE COURSES

The National Training and Development Institute (NTDI) is Ireland's largest non-Government training organisation with forty-six centres throughout Ireland catering for over 2000 students annually. There are no formal entry qualifications to any NTDI courses. Applicants must be over sixteen, be eligible for European Social Fund funding and be approved by the National Rehabilitation Board (NRB). The NRB will consider applications from dyslexic students.

For the severely affected dyslexic student who is having enormous difficulty coping with the demands of second-level school, these courses provide a route to qualifications and skills. All the courses are certified by outside examination bodies.

LEAVING CERTIFICATE

The ESRI study showed that more students are staying on in school after the Junior Certificate. In 1981 60% of students had some form of Senior Certificate. By 1995 this figure was 82%.

Since 1995 there are three types of Leaving Certificate being provided for students in senior cycle.

◆ The traditional Leaving Certificate. Here students do a two-year course of study and there is a final examination at the end of the two years. Most students take seven subjects. Subjects are offered at two levels, higher and ordinary. In Irish and Maths, foundation level is also offered. It would be expected that a student who did foundation level in these two subjects for Junior Certificate would take this level, as well as students who found the subjects exceptionally difficult at senior level. *Foundation level Maths and Irish are not acceptable for entry to many third-level courses and to some careers such as Nursing.* A decision that a student should take foundation level maths might be made in second year. The student and his parents often may not realise that the consequence of this decision which is that the student is not eligible for courses in the Institutes of Technology and Regional Technical Colleges after Leaving Certificate.

◆ Leaving Certificate Applied Programme (LCAP). This is a two year self-contained programme replacing the Senior Certificate and VPT courses. Its objective is to prepare participants for adult and working life. It has three main elements:

• Vocational preparation which focuses on the preparation for work, work experience, enterprise and communications.

• Vocational education which gives students general life skills, including the arts, social education, leisure and languages.

• General education which is concerned with the development of mathematical, information technology and practical skills necessary for specialist areas such as tourism, business, horticulture, engineering and technology.

Students are assessed throughout the two years, they receive credit for completing modules of the course and there are exams at the end of the two years. After finishing the course, the students could go on to employment or to PLC courses. Since they have not sat a traditional Leaving Certificate examination, they are not eligible to apply for CAO courses directly as the points system does not apply to the LCAP. However a student could do a LCAP, go on to a PLC and then, on the basis of the PLC qualification, apply to the Regional Technical Colleges through the CAO system. The LCAP was offered in over a hundred schools in 1996 and the Department of Education and Science has details of schools where it is offered.

◆ Leaving Certificate Vocational Programme (LCVP). The objective of this programme is to strengthen the vocational dimension of the Leaving Certificate through relating and integrating specific pairings of subjects. There are link modules to increase the vocational focus of the Leaving Certificate. The student will take a minimum of five subjects and these will include Irish and a foreign language. Subjects which complement one another will be grouped together and the student will take a particular group of subjects e.g. Engineering and Technical Drawing, Home Economics and Biology. There will be link modules covering preparation for work, work experience and enterprise education. As the student sits the Leaving Certificate examination he can apply to CAO at the end of the LCVP. LCVP was available in over 150 schools in 1996 and the Department of Education and Science has the list of schools which now offer it. If the student is interested in applying for CAO, check if the LCVP course will have five or six Leaving Certificate subjects. Six subjects are counted for points so taking five subjects may put the student at a disadvantage. The Regional Technical Colleges, the Nursing Application Centre and the Gardai accept the work experience and enterprise education module as a Leaving Certificate subject. When applying to the Regional Technical Colleges, a pass grade in the link module is worth 30 points, a merit grade 50 points and a distinction grade 70 points.

In my view unless there are particular circumstances, the preferable option for the vast majority of students is a Leaving Certificate of some type, apprenticeship or, if appropriate, a NTDI course. The other options do not provide the same amount of opportunity to equip a student for a career.

SUBJECT CHOICE FOR SENIOR CYCLE

This is a key moment in career choice for students. In Ireland, because students can take seven subjects or more for the Leaving Certificate, it is still possible to leave many paths open and not narrow one's options after the Junior Certificate. This is generally a good thing as it gives students time to mature before making critical career decisions. In the U.K. this is the time when students specialise and take a narrow range of subjects for A levels.

However, in Ireland where such a wide choice of subjects is offered, students with SLD may be at a disadvantage. They may have to take subjects which are language based and they may not be able to specialise in their best subjects. As an example of this, take a SLD student who is very proficient in the Maths, Business and Technical subjects. This student may have to take English, Irish and a third language as three of his seven subjects. Unless the option structure is very open, it is possible he may have to take other verbally based subjects such as Economics or History. If the same student could choose subjects such as English, Maths, Physics, Chemistry, Accounting, Technical Graphics and Engineering, it would certainly improve his chances of gaining points for the CAO system as well as giving him subjects he may enjoy studying.

I have always enjoyed working with students as they face the challenge of choosing senior cycle options. It is a time when one sees the adult emerging in the student as he faces up to making major decisions. Some students can be very mature and have very clear ideas, so subject choice is relatively simple. Others, while they have begun to think about careers, are not ready to narrow their options. It is important that these students do not limit their choice of careers. The Leaving Certificate provides a structure for students to maintain a wide choice. If a student is taking Irish (unless there is an exemption), English and Maths and chooses a language, a science and a business subject among his options, most careers and courses are open to him.

At this stage, when the student is making choices, parents and students need information on careers and course requirements. This is the time to start a careers file and begin research on colleges and courses. It is necessary to know the requirements for courses.

There are two sets of requirements:

♦ Colleges set minimum entry requirements. An example of this is the Regional Technical Colleges which set a requirement of five subjects in the Leaving Certificate with a pass grade in Maths and English or Irish for many of their courses. The four Colleges of NUI (UCC, UCD, UCG, and Maynooth) specify six subjects, two at Higher level, with a pass in English, Irish and a third language. If the SLD student has an exemption from Irish from the Department of Education, he is exempt from this Irish requirement. He can now also apply prior to entry to senior cycle to be exempt from the third language requirement. Full details are included in Appendix E. Trinity College Dublin and Limerick University require the student to have English and another language as an entry requirement.

◆ Certain courses have specific entry requirements. These are often related to what the student will be studying, e.g. a language course will specify that a student will need a certain grade in that language at Leaving Certificate.

Some examples of subject requirements include:

Maths   Higher level Maths is essential for Engineering degrees and Actuarial studies.
Ordinary level Maths is a minimum requirement for many Institute of Technology and Regional Technical College courses.

English   Higher level English is essential for Clinical Speech in TCD. Journalism in DCU and Communications in DCU.
Ordinary level English is required for a wide range of Institute of Technology and Regional Technical College courses.

Irish   Higher level Irish is essential for National Teacher training. Ordinary level Irish is required for entry in NUI colleges and nursing (unless Irish exemption applies).

Science   Science courses will require a science subject. TCD requires two sciences for some medical/paramedical courses. DIT requires higher level Chemistry for Dietetics.

Complete information on course requirements is available in the College brochures. These are available from the Admissions Office in each college.

The criteria for choosing subjects for Leaving Certificate should include:

◆ The student has the essential subjects needed for the courses he may consider doing after Leaving Certificate.

◆ He chooses subjects which will be of interest to him and that he will enjoy.

◆ If he is interested in applying for courses in the CAO system, he chooses subjects that will give him the best exam grades to maximise his points.

◆ In the case of the SLD student, the subjects should suit his profile of abilities and be subjects in which he can achieve.

Options after Leaving Certificate

Here again it is obvious from statistics that the longer the student remains in education the greater are the opportunities open to him. The ESRI survey published in December 1997 on the Economic Status of School-leavers shows that expanding economy has provided an increase in employment for school-leavers with Leaving Certificate qualifications since 1994. The survey also showed how the results in the Leaving Certificate can affect employment opportunities. The unemployment rate was 16.4% for school leavers with 5 D grades in the Leaving Certificate. It was down to 11.7% for students with four C grades on higher papers.

The choices available after Leaving Certificate are improving for all students including the SLD student. There is more employment, new courses, more places on courses, new routes to qualifications and the provision of more support services. It is a rapidly changing sector of education. Although it is often suggested that there is a shortage of places for students after Leaving Certificate, this is not the reality. There are a limited number of places on certain high demand courses such as Medicine, Law, Veterinary and Pharmacy. This scarcity of places raises the points for these courses. However there are plenty of places on courses available for school-leavers after the Leaving Certificate.

In 1997 65,000 students sat the Leaving Certificate. There were approximately 33,750 places available in the CAO system. There were another 17,000 places available in the PLC system. So, between the PLC and CAO systems, there were places in further education for over 75% of the Leaving Certificate group. This does not include the other application systems open to students such as Nursing, CERT, Teagasc, the U.K. colleges and the private colleges.

In recent years colleges at third-level have become more aware of SLD and the difficulties faced by SLD students. In my opinion there has been more development in support services at this level than at second-level.

Chapter 9 deals with the support systems offered by the various colleges in the CAO system. One example of new and very welcome developments in the provision of support services for such students is the National College of Art and Design's writing and research skills service. Many of the colleges have Disability Support Officers who give help, advice and support to SLD students. Some colleges accept SLD students as non-standard applicants (applicants who use pages 3 & 4 of the CAO form (see fig. 7.1) and would consider interviewing them as part of the selection process. Details on how to use this procedure are given in the CAO handbook. Some colleges may consider a waiver of minimum educational requirements in certain cases.

There are new routes to qualifications. PLC courses can lead on to certificate and diploma courses which can then lead on to degree courses. SLD students and their parents need to research widely so that they are informed about all the choices open to them.

The opportunities available at third-level are not only for students who get several honours in the Leaving Certificate. There were approximately one hundred courses at certificate level in the Regional Technical Colleges in 1997 which were offered at 200 points or below. This equates to a Leaving Certificate with one or two honours or high grades in pass subjects. Twenty courses were offered to all qualified applicants. In most cases this means a Leaving Certificate with five passes including Maths and English.

I know of a student with a one honour Leaving Certificate, who studied for the Certificate in Electronic Engineering, went on to do a Diploma in Electronic Engineering, transferred to Limerick University to obtain a degree and finished by doing a Master's. While this is rare, it is possible and the system is flexible enough for students to go as far as their abilities allow. This opens opportunities for the student with SLD. The student may not obtain the points to get on a degree course from his Leaving Certificate results, perhaps due to the number of verbally based subjects he has to take. He may obtain a place on a certificate level course. When he is studying a specialised topic which capitalises on his natural abilities, he may find it possible to progress to diploma and degree levels.

The main routes for a student seeking post Leaving Certificate qualifications are:

◆ The Central Applications Office (CAO): courses at degree, diploma and certificate level in Universities, Institutes of Technology, Regional Technical Colleges and other colleges.
◆ Post Leaving Certificate courses (PLCs).
◆ UCAS, the U.K. application system.

73

CAO

Page Two
Application Form 1998.

Application may be made for up to ten DEGREE courses and up to ten DIPLOMA/CERT courses by completing the appropriate section(s) below.
In both cases, courses should be entered in order of preference.
All of the third-level courses in the CAO system are categorised as either DEGREE or DIPLOMA/CERT.

Take special care NOT to mix DEGREE courses and DIPLOMA/CERT courses.

DEGREE SECTION

	Course Code	Course Reference
1		
2		
3		
4		
5		
6		
7		
8		
9		
10		

DIPLOMA/CERT SECTION

	Course Code	Course Reference
1		
2		
3		
4		
5		
6		
7		
8		
9		
10		

NOTE:

There are restrictions on the introduction of certain courses into an application for the first time after 1st February 1998. See Handbook pages 2 & 10 - 'Restricted-Application Courses'. In addition, individual admitting institutions may impose restrictions on certain categories of applicant. See Handbook page 5, final paragraph.

Is any Special Category, mentioned on page 3 of this Form, applicable in your case?
(WRITE 'Yes' or 'No' in the box on the right).

If you write 'No', do NOT enclose pages 3 and 4 in your application.

CAO

Page One
Application Form 1998.
(Complete in BLOCK LETTERS).

N.B. Read Pages 2, 3 and 4 of the Handbook before completing this Form.

SURNAME:

OTHER NAME(S):

TITLE (if desired)
(e.g. Ms., Mr., Rev., etc.):

Sex
(F or M):

Date of birth:
(ddmmyyyy):

Day Month Year

PERMANENT HOME ADDRESS:

Tel. No.:

COUNTRY OF BIRTH:

NATIONALITY:

ADDRESS FOR CORRESPONDENCE
(if different) :
(Note : Only one address may be shown here)

Tel.No.:

Name and address of second-level school(s) attended(latest first):

From: To:

19   19
19   19
19   19

If taking 1998 Leaving Cert. enter exam. number here.
Tick (√) if exam. number not yet supplied to you.

Leaving Cert.
98

(Leaving Cert. and N.U.I. Matric. examinations taken 1983 - 1997 inclusive).

Leaving Cert. exams.
1983-1997: ----------->

Year Exam. No.   Year Exam. No.   Year Exam. No.

N.U.I. Matric. exams.
1983-1992: ----------->

Year Exam. No.   Year Exam. No.   Year Exam. No.

(Enter details of other examinations/qualifications on Page Three).

I have read the regulations described in the CAO Handbook 1998 and in the CAO Application Form 1998 and I agree to be bound by them.

I affirm that the particulars given in this application are true and complete.

Signed:
(for pages 1 & 2)

Date:

Check   Office Use Only

Fig. 7.1   The CAO Form Pages 1 and 2

CAO

Page Four
Application Form 1998.

OFFICE USE ONLY

Date of Birth:

Name of applicant (surname, other names)

FURTHER DETAILS: Consult the Handbook page 3 and enter any prescribed further information relating to the Special Category/Categories which you have ticked on page 3. Number the information in the column on the left to correspond to the Category/Categories which you have ticked.

CAT. DETAILS

Signed (for pages 3 & 4):   Date:

CAO

Page Three
Application Form 1998.

OFFICE USE ONLY

Copy for:

Date of Birth:

Name of applicant (surname, other names)

Correspondence Address and Telephone Number.

INSTRUCTIONS: Pages 3 and 4 of the Handbook contain precise instructions about (i) the completion of pages 3 and 4 of this Form, (ii) the supply of certificates and other attachments and (iii) the supply of photocopies of pages 3 and 4 of this form and any attachments. These instructions are to ensure prompt consideration of your application; it is ESSENTIAL that you follow them exactly or the application will be returned to you and an extra fee will be imposed for its re-submission.

SPECIAL CATEGORY: Tick(√) whichever of the following applies in your case; it is essential to consult page 3 of the Handbook for information about completing this section. If more than one category applies, it is essential that you indicate this by ticking ALL of the appropriate boxes. Unticked boxes will be discounted. **In the case of Box 3, failure to disclose the appropriate information may result in the cancellation of the application. Checks are made to ensure that information has not been omitted.**

1.	SCE	2.	GC(S)E	3.	3RD LEVEL
4.	OTH S/L EXAM.	5.	NCVA/PLC	6.	TRADE/CRAFT
7.	MATURE	8.	SEQ	9.	D/H

GC(S)E EXAMS already taken. (Do **not** list subjects & results). Attach Certificates.

Month/Year	Board	Month/Year	Board	Month/Year	Board

GC(S)E EXAMS to be taken.

Board	School No	Candidate No	Subject	Level *	Board	School No.	Candidate No	Subject	Level *
NICCTEA									
NICCEA									
NICCTEA									
NICCTEA									

* Enter level as follows: A = Advanced; S = Advanced Supplementary; O = GCSE
Enter (M) after the level, if the subject is being taken under the modular system, e.g. A(M)

Fig. 7.1 The CAO Form Pages 3 and 4

- Colleges of further education in the U.K.
- Nursing.
- CERT, hotel, catering and tourism courses.
- Teagasc, agriculture and horticulture courses.
- Private colleges.
- FAS, apprenticeships and training courses.

THE CENTRAL APPLICATIONS OFFICE (CAO)

This is the main application system for Leaving Certificate students. It covers approximately 34,000 places on courses in thirty-eight colleges. It is a joint application system for degree, diploma and certificate level courses. In 1998 the following private colleges are included in the CAO for the first time: LSB, the American University and Portobello College. It is important to remember that fees are payable for courses in private colleges.

It is a single application form. The student can apply for up to ten degree courses and ten certificate/diploma courses; a total of twenty courses.

The CAO handbook sets out the precise application procedures to be followed and is available from the CAO. The important dates to remember are the closing date, 1st February and late closing date 1st May. If the student wishes to change his order of preference on the list of courses or to introduce new courses, there is a change of mind facility up to 1st July. There are a small number of courses that have additional selection procedures, such as aptitude tests or portfolios. These courses must be included prior to 1st February and it is not possible to introduce these courses on a change of mind slip. Offers of places are determined by points for the vast majority of courses provided the student satisfies the college entry requirements and any specified course requirements. Details of the points system are in Fig. 7.2. The points from the previous year can be used as a rough guide when looking at courses but the points are set each year by the number of places on the course and the number of applicants.

THE POINTS SYSTEM

I am not going to explain the precise details of the CAO system. Such information is contained in the CAO handbook. However there are some points relevant to SLD students.

- It is very important that decisions about colleges and courses are thoroughly researched. The student should collect relevant college brochures, attend open days, talk to the staff at the colleges and to students attending the courses. It means reading the brochures and

Leaving Certificate grade	higher paper	lower paper	bonus
A1	100	60	40
A2	90	50	35
B1	85	45	30
B2	80	40	25
B3	75	35	20
C1	70	30	15
C2	65	25	10
C3	60	20	5
D1	55	15	
D2	50	10	
D3	45	5	

The best six results are counted for points calculation. Bonus points for Higher Maths are awarded by the University of Limerick.

Fig. 7.2 The Points System

knowing the content of the courses in which the student is interested. The same course title can differ in content from college to college. An example of this is the National Certificate in Business Studies. In some colleges it includes languages and in others it does not.

◆ Chapter 9 gives details of the support services offered by the various third level colleges. Colleges vary in the support they offer SLD students.

◆ Ask the college about waiving minimum requirements if you think this may be necessary and appropriate. Some colleges will consider such a waiver.

◆ Use the CAO system fully. This means applying for the twenty courses allowed between both lists. **It is important that choices be in order of preference the entire way down each list.** Do not restrict yourself to one location. It is a very noticeable trend that Dublin students do not apply on a national basis but tend to apply to Dublin colleges only. They place themselves at a disadvantage in so doing. The points for courses in Dublin are usually higher than for the same course at a Regional Technical College outside the Dublin area. Take the case of a student interested in Electronics. At degree level in 1997 the points ranged from 480 for Engineering in UCC to 315 for an Electronics degree in Waterford. At certificate level, the points ranged from 290 for Electronic Engineering in DIT to courses where all qualified applicants (those with five passes including English and Maths) got places. On the degree list the student should put the courses he wants in order of preference. This is the most important instruction in filling in the form. He could then use his ninth and tenth preference for courses he may consider if his Leaving Certificate results are lower than he expects. For example, he may want to do an engineering degree in Dublin and will list these courses among his top preferences. He may then consider including courses with lower points as a lower preference. On the certificate/diploma list the student should put the courses he wants in order of preference but again use the ninth and tenth choices for courses that need fewer points.

◆ Points do not give a ranking to how good a course is. They are a reflection of the number of students applying for that particular course in a particular year. Remember points will vary from year to year but there are patterns to be seen. One pattern is that students prefer to take courses in large cities which have a thriving student population. In the case of the National Certificate in Computing, the same qualification is offered in many of the Regional Technical Colleges. The student may need more points to get a place in Dublin, Cork or Galway and yet the student who studies in other colleges will have the same qualification. The points for certain types of courses may reflect the perception that students hold of employment prospects after the course. An example of such a trend is engineering degree courses for which the points dropped during the 1980's and have risen sharply in the 1990's.

◆ Even if the student feels confident about obtaining a CAO place, he could also apply to PLC courses as a precaution. He can turn down courses in September but he may not be able to apply for them at this stage. So the student should apply for a PLC in Electronics with the idea that if he does not get a CAO place, he could do a PLC course. It may be possible to apply to CAO the following year using his PLC results.

◆ The CAO structure is very flexible at certificate/diploma level. Students can do a two-year certificate. If they obtain the necessary results they can do one more year and get a diploma. In the Regional Technical Colleges it may also be possible to do a further year of study after the diploma to obtain a degree qualification. A list of these add-on degrees is in Appendix A.

◆ It might also be possible to transfer to university after completing a national certificate or diploma. The transfer is based on the student's results but it applies to certain faculties only, such as Business Studies, Science and Engineering.

◆ ACCS is a system which allows part-time students acquire nationally recognised qualifications in the Regional Technical Colleges. This can provide another route to qualifications.

POST LEAVING CERTIFICATE COURSES

This is a rapidly developing sector of education. Each year more courses are added to the list and existing courses are further developed. These developments include links to other educational institutions both here and in Britain. While the vast majority of these courses is aimed at the pass Leaving Certificate student who is not likely to get a CAO place, some have such a high reputation that they could be a student's first option regardless of what CAO place he is offered.

These courses have been designed to prepare students for the world of work and often reflect local employment opportunities. It is also possible for students who have successfully completed PLC courses to obtain a place on certificate level courses in the CAO system. PLC courses are available in a wide variety of colleges throughout the country. There is a list of main PLC colleges in Appendix B.

Students must apply individually to each college. There is no centralised system. Many of the colleges have open days usually in February and March each year. There is an open day for all the City of Dublin PLC colleges in March each year. Applications will be accepted from January onwards or at the open days. Closing dates also can vary. Some, particularly for courses with a high demand for places, can be as early as March. However there can be places available on some courses as late as September.

The selection procedures differ and include interviews, aptitude tests or the presentation of a portfolio. Some courses are in very high demand, particularly where the college is running a unique course such as the Colaiste Dhulaigh Communications course or the Ballyfermot Senior College Animation course. The most common selection procedure is an interview. A portfolio will be needed when applying for Art and Design courses. For Communication, Radio and TV courses, relevant experience which may take the form of a portfolio is desirable. For Journalism, a portfolio of published material is useful.

Since it can be an interview system, this may suit the SLD student who may not have very good grades in the Leaving Certificate but who is articulate and who has gained relevant experience. After Junior Certificate, the student should begin to develop his C.V. Work experience, achievements in sport, contribution to the community and award schemes such as An Gaisce (the President's Award Scheme), all can help at interview.

There is a vast range of courses in this sector. Some are available at many of the PLC colleges, some are unique to one college. They can be classified into main groups as follows:

Art, Craft, Design	Art, Craft, Design, Fashion Design, Interior Design, Computer Aided Design, Furniture Restoration, Animation.
Business	Business, Secretarial, Computer Applications, Marketing, Languages, Retail Studies, Auctioneering, Security.
Science, Technology and Natural Resources	Laboratory Techniques, Horticulture, Motor Technology, Food Science, Construction, Electronics Technology, Equestrian Studies.
Services, Leisure and Tourism	Hotel, Catering, Tourism, Beauty, Child Care, Nursing Studies, Hairdressing, Tennis Coaching, Marine Skills, Leisure Management, Football, Heritage Studies.
Communications	Advertising, Journalism, Communications, Video Production, Performing Arts, Languages.

The National Council for Vocational Awards (NCVA) has been set up to provide a certification system for vocational education courses. In the past a wide variety of Bodies/Institutes has acted as certifying organisations. The NCVA, it is hoped, will bring greater coherence to the system. The NCVA will make awards at four levels. Most PLC courses will be offered at Level 2. The standards of certification will apply nationally. This will facilitate mobility between different educational levels and allow integration with European systems of vocational qualifications. However some PLC courses do not have NCVA recognition. This should be checked in the brochures.

The Regional Technical Colleges recognise and give credit for NCVA Level 2 courses. In 1997 approximately 1,000 places on certificate level courses were reserved for students with NCVA Level 2 qualifications covering the entire spectrum from Art and Design to Business and from Science and Computers to Engineering. Applicants for these places use pages 3 & 4 of the CAO form. Places are allocated on the results of the PLC course. The grade-point average over the eight modules of the PLC course will decide how places are allocated.

Besides the NCVA certification, some courses have recognition from professional bodies such as the Professional Accountancy Bodies or they receive certification from organisations such as City and Guilds. Some courses award British Higher National Diplomas. Some of the courses allow the student, after successfully completing the PLC, to transfer to a British University.

These courses have been designed to prepare students for the world of work. On completing the course, students can take different routes such as:

◆ Go directly into the labour market.
◆ Continue in education through a CAO application to the Regional Technical Colleges.
◆ Continue in education through the U.K. system. Some PLC courses have already established a direct link to further qualification, e.g. the horticultural course in St. Peter's, Killester has a direct link to Writtle College, Chelmsford.

Usually there are no course fees, although examination and administration fees may have to be paid. Maintenance grants are due to be introduced for PLC courses from September 1998. These grants are means tested.

Applying to Colleges in the UK System

There is a centralised application system in the UK for both degree and diploma places at university. It is for all the universities including the former polytechnics. It is called UCAS (University and College Admissions Service).

The closing date for applications is 15th December, except in the case of Oxford and Cambridge universities when the closing date is 15th October. Students fill in the form and list up to six courses. These courses are not in order of preference (except for Art and Design courses). The system differs from the CAO in that personal information is included on the form. On a page included as part of the form, the student can state his reasons for choosing these courses, his relevant work experience, relevant school subjects and his achievements. The form is passed on to an academic referee, usually a designated teacher in his school, who will write a confidential reference on the student covering points such as ability, achievement, potential, contribution to school life, disability and a forecast of Leaving Certificate results. The referee posts the form to UCAS.

UCAS send a copy of the form to each college to which the student applied. Each college considers the application and may make a conditional offer. The conditional offer will specify the academic goals to be achieved in the Leaving Certificate. The student will know in March or April what results he will need to achieve in the Leaving Certificate to ensure his place on a course. The academic goals set out in each offer may differ depending on the demand for places on the particular course. While the student may receive six offers, he can accept two only. The student may choose a college which has set high academic goals in the Leaving Certificate as a firm acceptance and hold a lower offer as insurance in case he does not get the results he hopes for in the Leaving Certificate

For degree level courses, colleges generally look for four Leaving Certificate honours subjects as a minimum qualification. For diploma courses the minimum entry qualifications can be less. Courses are offered at levels much above this minimum qualification, depending on the course, the reputation of the university and the geographical location of the college.

At the moment there are no fees for EU citizens for the vast majority of courses. A recent report on higher education in the U.K. recommended tuition fees of up to £1,000 per annum be introduced from 1998.

Students, who are eligible for Irish Higher Education maintenance grants, can avail of these grants while they attend most courses in the U.K. There are some exceptions to this, so be careful to check that the courses chosen are eligible. Irish Higher Education grants are means-tested..

There are over 80,000 courses in the UCAS system which include subjects and subject combinations not available here. There is no change of mind facility as there is in the CAO system. This means there is a greater need for detailed research before filling in the form. Students need to know as much as possible about the courses and colleges to which they are applying. Since applications are submitted in October/November prior to the Leaving Certificate, this research should be started during fifth year.

Reasons why SLD students may consider applying to the U.K.:
◆ Although for high demand courses such as Law, Medicine, Veterinary and Pharmacy entry standards are as high in the U.K. as they are in

Ireland, the entrance standards on more general courses such as Computers, Business Studies, Languages and Engineering may be lower than the equivalent course on the CAO system. One reason for this is the different population structure. In Ireland there is more demand for college places because of the very high proportion of young people in our population.

♦ There is more awareness of dyslexia in the U.K. and colleges make more support systems available. While there is no information database about U.K. support systems available yet, I know of one SLD student at one London College who was given a laptop computer as a support system. There is a National Working Party on Dyslexia in Higher Education based in the University of Hull, which is in the process of compiling a report on existing provision for assessment and support of dyslexic students.

♦ There is a wider range of courses and options within courses available in the U.K.

♦ The Irish application procedure does not allow for information about the student to be included unless one applies as a non-standard applicant. The U.K. procedure allows for other information both in the student's personal statement and the academic reference. The decision to make an offer takes this information into account. This could be of benefit to a SLD student.

♦ Many Irish applicants use the U.K. system as a form of insurance in case they do not get the place they want in Ireland.

Other sources of information on the U.K. system include:

♦ The British Council in Dublin will answer queries on U.K. courses.

♦ Philomena Ott's book *How to detect and manage Dyslexia* contains a detailed chapter on further and higher education in the U.K.

♦ SKILL is an organisation in the U.K. similar to AHEAD in Ireland which is concerned about the needs of students with disabilities. It has many publications which could be helpful.

♦ There is a CD Rom called Ecctis, which is a database of all the courses in the UCAS system. It is available in some schools and Youth Information Offices.

♦ In September each year the Institute of Guidance Counsellors, in conjunction with the Irish Times, organise the Higher Options Conference in the R.D.S., Dublin. Many British colleges as well as Irish colleges are represented. It is advisable that students attend this conference. It is held over three days. An information night for parents is held during the conference.

Colleges of Further Education

These are colleges all over the U.K. offering diploma or certificate level qualifications in the fields of Engineering, Computer, Business, Social Care, Art, Catering, Leisure or Teaching. Contact the colleges individually to see the application procedure.

NURSING

There are about 1000 training places available annually in the nursing schools. Information about nursing in Ireland is available from An Bord Altranais.

The entry requirements for nursing are:

◆ Applicants must be 17 years old on 1st June in the year they apply. Six subjects in the Leaving Certificate are needed, two of which must be Grade C3 or higher on the honours paper and four at Grade D3 or higher on the ordinary level paper. Subjects should include English, Maths, Irish (unless exempt by the Department of Education) and a science subject. A European language is also required. Foundation level Maths and Irish are not acceptable

Rapid changes are occurring in nurse training. An Bord Altranais will have details of any developments. In 1997 application for nurse training for the vast majority of training schools was made to the Nursing Applications Centre, P.O. Box 5711 Dublin 2. The closing date was 16.5.97. It is hoped that all training schools will be included in this centralised system in 1998. The courses lead to registration as a nurse with An Bord Altranais and the award of a Diploma in Nursing from a third-level institution. A further one-year academic programme leading to a degree in nursing is offered by the third-level institutions. This is an optional choice.

There are three types of nurse training available in Ireland.

◆ General nursing is concerned with the provision of total nursing care for the sick and physically injured.

◆ Psychiatric Nursing is concerned with caring for people with psychiatric illnesses.

◆ Mental handicapped nursing is concerned with children and adults with a mental handicap.

There are many pre-nursing courses and child care courses available in the PLC sector. Check out PLC colleges (Appendix B). The pre-nursing course will give relevant work experience and information about nursing. Students will still need the minimum Leaving Certificate requirements. Some PLC courses allow the option of doing some Leaving Certificate subjects in conjunction with the pre-nursing course. This would be of benefit to a student who did not obtain the necessary grades for entry to nursing in the Leaving Certificate.

There is a dental nursing course in the Dental Hospital in TCD. Applications are made directly to the college.

The addresses to write to for information about nursing in the U.K. are:

Northern Ireland	National Board for Nursing, RAC House, 79 Chilchester Street, Belfast BT1 4JE.
Scotland	National Board for Nursing, 22 Queen Street, Edinburgh EH2 1JX.
Wales	National Board for Nursing, Floor 13, Pearl Assurance House Greyfriars Road, Cardiff CF1 3AG
England	National Board for Nursing, Careers Section P.O. Box 2EN London W1A 2EN.

The entry requirements for students from Ireland are five passes in the Leaving Certificate; grades must be D or higher on higher papers or C or higher on ordinary papers. If a student does not reach this standard, there is the UKCC Educational (DC) test, which assesses the applicants' aptitude for nursing and can be taken three times. Passing this test means the applicant is eligible for nurse training. Candidates can prepare for this test at Cavan College of Further Studies and Kildare College for Further Studies.

HOTEL, CATERING AND TOURISM COURSES

CERT is the state training agency for hotels, catering and tourism. It advertises application procedures and closing dates for courses in January each year.

For most courses students need to be seventeen and to have passed their Leaving Certificate.

CERT provide courses for the following:

◆ Chef.
◆ Accommodation Assistant.
◆ Waiter/Waitress.
◆ Hospitality Assistant.
◆ Bartender.

◆ Tourism Information Assistant.

◆ Hotel Receptionist.

Many PLC colleges offer CERT Level 2 courses throughout the country. These courses give students basic skills in tourism, catering and hotel work.

There are nine courses in hotel and catering management provided through the CAO system at degree, diploma and certificate level. Shannon College of Hotel Management is a private college which provides a four-year diploma in hotel management. Ballyfermot Senior College has a PLC course in hotel management. The Northern Ireland Hotel and Catering College, Portrush, runs a variety of hotel and catering courses.

AGRICULTURE

Teagasc offers a range of agricultural and horticultural courses throughout the country. There are eleven agricultural colleges.

Courses offered include:

◆ The Certificate in Agriculture.

◆ The Certificate in Farming, with six options including general agriculture, horse production, agri-forestry, pig production and commercial horticulture.

◆ Farm management training.

◆ Amenity horticulture, based in the National Botanic Gardens, Glasnevin, Dublin 9.

◆ Horticultural skills course in Multyfarnham, Co. Westmeath.

◆ Farm machinery.

Further information on these courses is available from Teagasc. Applications are made directly to the colleges, which host open days in May each year.

PRIVATE COLLEGES

There are a growing number of private colleges offering courses to students. The majority of the courses offered deal with business and accounting. It is very important to check the validation given to the qualification offered. Several have NCEA recognition. The NCEA is the body which validates the awards from the Regional Technical Colleges. Some of the courses are included in the CAO system for the first time in 1998. For the rest students apply directly to the college. Fees are charged for these course. Tax relief is available on fees paid on some courses.

There may be an interview system for assessing applicants. Class sizes may be smaller than in the larger colleges. See appendix C for a list of the main private colleges.

FAS TRAINING COURSES

Apprenticeship training has been dealt with Chapter 6. FAS also, through its training centre network, provides close on 170 different training courses of an industrial and commercial nature for unemployed workers, those wishing to update their skills or change their careers and for school-leavers unable to obtain employment.

FAS courses are available to men and women who are unemployed, redundant or out of full-time education. All applicants for FAS courses must register with their local FAS employment services offices.

Training allowances are paid to trainees. Accommodation costs are subsidised for those who must live away from home during the course. For further information, contact the local FAS employment services offices or training centre.

Institute of Horology, Mill Road, Blanchardstown, Dublin 15, offers a Diploma in Watchmaking.

Choosing a Career Direction

8

The nature of the job market in the 1990's means students are better equipped if they have further training or education of some sort after the Leaving Certificate. This is why the major decision for students in their last year at second-level is what courses should they apply for to continue their education.

There is rapid change and developments in the courses provided after the Leaving Certificate. Sometimes in speaking to parents, I am aware that their view of colleges and courses has remained fairly static since the time that they themselves were at school and they still hold the opinions about colleges and qualifications that they held then. This means they can lack an understanding of the complexities and the flexibility of the choices available to-day. Even as a guidance counsellor it is a major challenge to stay up-to-date with the constant innovation in courses. To be properly informed, parents need to make themselves aware of the major changes. Some of these changes include:

- ◆ The growing reputation of Institutes of Technology and Regional Technical Colleges. In some cases employers would look first to these colleges rather than the traditional universities.
- ◆ The growth in add-on degrees in the Regional Technical College sector (see Appendix A). This may not be apparent from the CAO handbook which lists the certificate/diploma level courses. The possibility is open from many of these courses to do a degree after successfully completing the diploma examination.
- ◆ The growth in Post Leaving Certificate courses has been astronomical, both in the number and range of courses provided.
- ◆ The increasing flexibility and adaptability of the system so students can move from Post Leaving Certificate course to national certificate, to national diploma and on to degree level. This provides alternative routes to qualifications.

◆ The introduction of systems such as ACCS to help the part-time student acquire qualifications which are fully certified by the NCEA.

Because of the number of courses and alternative routes to qualifications, students and parents need to research courses. It is not something that should be left to sixth year. It can be difficult to make students realise the urgency in becoming informed about courses and to begin research. It is very frustrating to go through the CAO system in detail in the classroom in November and then to have some students wake up in mid-January and come and ask questions about the system when the closing date for applications is 1st February.

The first place to start the research is with the guidance counsellor in the school, who will be able to provide information about colleges, courses, open days and application procedures. The level of provision of a careers service can vary from school to school depending on whether there is a guidance counsellor and the number of hours that are allocated to guidance counselling. Since the guidance counsellor works within the school, he/she will have a good knowledge of the student's abilities, interests and possible results.

Further information can be gained from newspapers particularly around mid-August and mid-January. However there can an element of hyped-up information and headlines can tend to centre around courses where points have risen or around the handful of courses that require 500 plus points. Outside the louder headlines, the papers do contain excellent information and sometimes information which is not available elsewhere. This is because of the rapid change in the nature of courses provided and in the job market itself. Publications tend to go out-of-date very quickly. These articles are often accompanied by large advertisements about colleges and courses. Remember that the colleges in highest demand do not need to advertise heavily!

Students should open a careers file and keep all the relevant information in it.

Open days are held from September on. Some schools organise trips to visit colleges. The Institute of Guidance Counsellors prepares a list of the main open days in September each year. Some of the major open days or information days are:

◆ The Higher Options Conference in late-September organised by the Irish Times and the Institute of Guidance Counsellors. Most Irish colleges and many U.K. colleges attend and there is a parents' session one evening.

◆ In February FAS, in conjunction with the Institute of Guidance Counsellors and the Irish Independent, organise a three-day seminar on careers and employment trends which includes lectures and displays.

◆ DIT runs a series of lectures at night during October and November. Each night focuses on a particular group of courses. DIT also host an open day in January.

◆ UCD runs open days in mid-March with over 20,000 students attending.

◆ DCU runs an open day on the third Saturday in November.

◆ Trinity College, NCAD and Mater Dei have open days in December.

◆ University of Limerick has an open day in January.

◆ Most of the Regional Technical Colleges have open days.

◆ PLC colleges hold open days during the months of February and March.

◆ The agricultural colleges have open days in May.

If the student or parents are interested in a particular college, ring the college and ask if there is to be an open day. Even if there is not, the staff in the various colleges often make the time available to talk to individual interested students.

Work experience can be another invaluable way to obtain information about careers. I would encourage students to look for work experience during transition year or the summers following transition year or fifth year. It can help them choose a career direction and be of positive benefit if there is an interview for the course.

Of course the key questions are: what courses will students research? What careers interests them? The answer to these questions lie in a process which begins soon after they enter second-level. Some of the constituent factors in making the decision are:

◆ Ability. Each student has a different profile of ability. A test used very much in Irish Schools is DATS (Differential Aptitude Testing) which gives a percentile score based on national norms of a student's ability in Verbal Reasoning, Numeric Reasoning, Abstract Reasoning, Spatial Relations, Mechanical Reasoning, Clerical Speed and Accuracy, Spelling and Grammar. In the case of SLD students psychological assessments provide much more detailed information on the student's ability. These could be even more relevant than the DATS. If the student's profile either from DATS or a psychological assessment has particular strengths and weaknesses, career choices should be centred on the strengths. The SLD student with difficulties in spelling and verbal expression would be wise to avoid careers where verbal skills are important such as office work or journalism. It appears to be a pattern that many SLD students have a strength in spatial relations. This could lead into art, architecture, engineering or design.

◆ Achievement. Achievement is different from ability. Some students with seemingly low levels of ability can achieve very good results if they have perseverance and motivation to focus on their studies. Other students with excellent ability can do quite badly. A pattern of achievement can be built up by monitoring school reports. Expectations of results in state exams can be based on this. It is highly unlikely that a student who is achieving the grades of 'E' and 'D' during fifth year and sixth year will jump to grades of 'A' and 'B' in the Leaving Certificate examination. For most students their grades will be close to their level of achievement in school. This makes it possible to predict the probable range of results in state examinations that a student may achieve. This information can form part of the career decision and helps to make the choice realistic. If a student's results in house exams are around 250 points, the estimated range of the Leaving Certificate results could be between 200 to 350. It is realistic for the student to ensure courses in this range are included on the CAO application. In the CAO system where there are 20 choices to be made, the student may still use some of those choices for courses that may go for 400 plus points but he should also ensure he has courses in the range of 200 points.

◆ Interest Testing. These are tests which ask the students questions about careers and indicate their level of interest in different career groups. These tests are often used at the stage of option choice for senior cycle.

◆ Included in some of the interest testing can be questions about the students' interests and personality such as: What do they like to do with their spare time? Do they like to work as part of a team? Do they enjoy organising events? Would they prefer to spend their time mending machines or playing sports or board games? Do they like activities that help care for people such as First Aid or visiting elderly relatives?

◆ Other achievements outside the academic: Have they been involved in sports teams, First Aid, drama, life-saving, sailing or music? How proficient are they in these activities? Do they want this activity to continue as part of their career? Do they have a driving licence?

Sometimes leisure interests and achievements provide a route to a career choice.

◆ Work experience will also give students ideas about the type of work they would like to pursue or avoid in the future. It will also provide them with a reference which may be useful at interviews later on.

All these threads; achievement, ability, interests, personality, work experience and other non-academic achievement, form a realistic basis to the process of career decision. It should also provide a list of possible career directions that the student would like to research further. Once the student begins to research the courses available and different routes to qualifications, his ideas will be further refined. It is a process that will take time and should be ongoing during all of senior cycle. Preferably it will have started sooner.

Occasionally students will present in sixth year as having no idea as to what career interests them. This can provide a serious obstacle to a discussion. However if presented with a list of broad career groupings, they have very clear ideas about careers they do not want to pursue and it is possible to reduce the list to maybe six broad career headings which they might consider. This provides a good starting point for research.

The above discussion on career choice focuses on the individual's aptitudes, interests and achievements. Another factor to consider is employment trends. These are notoriously unpredictable. This is because of the changing nature of jobs due to technology and the global market. There are many jobs being advertised now which were not in existence ten years ago. However there are some patterns discernible:

◆ There is employment growth in the Irish Economy which is very welcome as it provides more opportunities for school-leavers. The students who will benefit most will the students with qualifications and/or good skills.

◆ Certain sectors of the economy are providing major employment prospects. These include:
  • Computer and electronics.
  • Hotel, catering and tourism.
  • Food science and technology.
  • Telemarketing, particularly with language skills.
  • Manufacturing technology.
  • Engineering.
  • Telecommunications.

◆ There is going to be more contract work and fewer permanent appointments. The rapidly growing and confident economy that now exists in Ireland provides the encouraging environment for qualified and skilled workers to set up their own businesses. This is an increasingly attractive option given the growing impermanence of employment.

◆ Because of the developments in technology and resulting changes in job practices, there is a great need for adaptability and flexibility. Workers will need to constantly up-date their skills and information.

Up-to-date information on career trends appears in the newspapers usually in August and January, both critical times for course choices. The FAS seminar in February discusses trends in employment. It makes sense that information on employment trends would be part of a decision on career direction.

Support Services Offered by Third-Level Colleges

9

In March 1997 a survey was carried out on the support services provided to the SLD students at third-level. A questionnaire was sent to the admissions officers in the institutions participating in the CAO system. Questions were grouped into four sections: admissions policy, the incidence of dyslexia among the student body, support services offered to students both in normal college activities and in exams. Twenty four colleges replied. The responses received are given below. The colleges are listed in alphabetical order. It was very evident from reading some of the replies that there was a very positive desire to help such students.

All Hallows College
All Hallows is a small college and as yet has not had students present with dyslexic difficulties. The college does not yet have an explicit policy with regard to students with special needs although in the past it has looked sympathetically at individual applications and has made every effort to facilitate such applications.

Colaiste Mhuire, Marino
There are no dyslexic students in a student body of one hundred and sixty-five students. The college admits dyslexic students to its courses. The college will not waive minimum entry requirements as these are set by the Department of Education. The college has an assessment policy for students who become aware they may have dyslexia while at third-level. The college policy is one of openness and support to such students, if any should gain admission.

Cork Institute of Technology
There are approximately 4,300 students attending the college. The college admits dyslexic students to all courses. In the case of Nautical Science and

Marine Engineering there is a medical test to be passed. The college would consider waiving minimum entry requirements. The student can apply to the college as a non-standard applicant on the CAO form. If the student applies as a non-standard applicant, he/she would automatically be offered a place if he/she obtains the entry qualifications and points (in the case of restricted courses, the special entrance tests must be passed).

The college does provide a support service for dyslexic students which includes:

♦ Photocopying of lecture notes.
♦ Use of a tape recorder in lectures by arrangement with the lecturer.
♦ Provision of a computer for lectures, library work, etc., if required.

The college makes the following facilities available in exams if necessary:

♦ Use of an amanuensis (scribe).
♦ Use of a reader.
♦ Use of a word processor.
♦ The facility to tape exams or take them orally.
♦ The facility to use a dictionary, thesaurus or spellmaster.
♦ The provision of extra time in the exam.
♦ Scripts are labelled so examiners know the student is dyslexic.

The college does provide information in increase the awareness of dyslexia among the student body.

Dublin City University

Dublin City University is committed to facilitating people with disabilities as an issue of basic human rights and an integral part of its commitment to equality of opportunity in higher education.

Applicants with a disability can choose to apply for their primary degree programme by direct application. The closing date for such applications is April 2nd on the year of entry. Direct applications must be supported by details of the nature and degree of the disability to ensure that the student's requirements can be catered for.

The university has a disability liaison officer who is responsible for the development and implementation of the university's equal opportunities policy for people with disabilities.

DCU provides the following support services on request:

♦ Free photocopying (subject to reasonable limits).
♦ Lecturer's notes.
♦ Provision of materials prior to lectures.
♦ Access to computers and computer software packages.

- Reading service and books on tape.
- Extra tuition.
- Individual arrangements for exams.
- Assistance in using the library.

Dublin Institute of Technology

There are 24,000 students attending DIT (full-time and part-time). There is no accurate figure on the number of diagnosed dyslexics attending. DIT admits dyslexic students to all courses. If a student becomes aware of dyslexic difficulties while attending DIT, in-house psychological assessment may be made available and also referral to an external educational psychologist which is funded by the student services office.

The Institute provides the following support services:

- Provision of members of staff to act as support officer and access officer.
- Provision of special courses, workshops and study skills seminars.
- Photocopying of lecture notes.
- Use of a tape recorder in lectures.
- Provision of the following computer facilities: talking PCs, laptops, PC software (text-help) and magnification systems.

The Institute makes the following available if necessary in exams:

- Use of an amanuensis (scribe).
- Use of a reader.
- The facility to tape exams or take them orally.
- The facility to use a dictionary, thesaurus or spellmaster.
- The provision of extra time in exams.

The Institute provides information to academic staff and staff development programmes on dyslexia as well as information to increase awareness of dyslexia among students.

Froebel College of Education, Sion Hill

There are no dyslexic students in the student body of one hundred and forty students.

The college does not admit dyslexic students to the Bachelor in Education degree for primary school teachers. The college follows the Department of Education guidelines for minimum entry requirements. Since the college has no dyslexic students, it does not provide a support service. It does provide information to increase awareness of dyslexia among students.

Mary Immaculate College, Limerick

There are two diagnosed dyslexic students in a student body of 1,300. Entry to the Bachelor of Education is governed by the Department of Education requirements. The college has an assessment policy for students who may become aware of dyslexic difficulties while at third-level.

The college provides a support service for dyslexic students which includes:

◆ Provision of a member of staff to act as a support officer.

◆ Photocopying of lecture notes.

◆ Use of a tape recorder in lectures.

◆ Provision of computer facilities including talking PCs and laptops.

The college makes the following facilities available in exams if necessary:

◆ Use of a word processor.

◆ The provision of extra time in exams.

Information is provided to all academic staff on dyslexia.

Mater Dei Institute of Education

There are no dyslexic students at present in a student body of two hundred and thirty undergraduates. The college has one undergraduate course and admits dyslexic students to that course depending on the needs of the student.

The college accepts NUI or Trinity College matriculation standards. Trinity College does not require the student to have a third language. The student, when applying for a place in Mater Dei, should tick the health/disability box on page three and complete page four of the CAO form and would then be assessed on points. They would be invited to come for interview, however, so that in the case of their getting the required points, the college would know if it could meet their needs as a dyslexic. The interview is therefore essential.

The college does provide a support service for dyslexic students, depending on the degree of dyslexia. There is a member of staff who acts as a support officer and dyslexic students do have access to a tutor trained in how dyslexia affects students at third-level.

The college makes the following available if necessary in exams:

◆ The college is open to providing the facility to tape exams or take them orally and to use a dictionary, thesaurus or spellmaster.

◆ The provision of extra time in exams.

◆ Labelling of scripts so examiners know the student has dyslexia.

The college is a small private college and has no dyslexic students at present. It has had some students in the past, with very mild forms of dyslexia, for whom it was able to provide the supports needed and both academic and administrative staff are very open to doing whatever is necessary to support students.

Milltown Institute of Theology and Philosophy
When surveyed there was one dyslexic student in a student body of two hundred and fifty. The college admits to all courses students registered as dyslexic. The college does not waive minimum entry requirements on the assumption that a 'formally assessed' student would have received compensatory consideration at Leaving Certificate.

The college provides a support service for students which includes:
◆ Photocopying of notes for all students.
◆ Use of tape recorder with the permission of the lecturer.
◆ Computer for lectures and library work.
◆ The college facilitates the application by students to the Department of Education for appropriate computer software and hardware for which there are grants available.

The college provides the following facilities if necessary in exams:
◆ Use of word processor (considered for each individual case).
◆ The facility to tape exams or take them orally.
◆ The provision of extra time in exams (considered on individual basis).
◆ Scripts are labelled so examiners know that the student has dyslexia.

Regional Technical College, Athlone
There are approximately 3000 students attending the college. Less than fifteen dyslexic students present themselves each year to the College Counsellor who co-ordinates the facilities made available to them.

The college admits dyslexic students to all courses. The student can apply as a non-standard applicant to be assessed independent of the points system. The assessment takes the form of an invitation to meet the relevant staff. The student, who applies as a non-standard applicant, is automatically offered a place if he satisfies the minimum entry requirements and points. The college counsellor will assess students who become aware they may have dyslexia while at third-level.

The college makes the following support services available:
◆ A counsellor is available to all students.
◆ Photocopying of lecture notes.
◆ Use of a tape recorder in lectures.
◆ PC software for dyslexics and spellmasters.

The college makes the following available in exams if necessary:
- Use of an amanuensis/scribe.
- Use of a word processor.
- The facility to tape mid-year assessments or take them orally.
- A marking allowance is given by staff when marking exam scripts.

The college currently provides information to staff on dyslexia and hopes to establish staff development programmes on dyslexia for all staff. The college also hopes to disseminate information on dyslexia among the student body.

Regional Technical College, Carlow.

In 1996/1997 three students identified themselves as being dyslexic in a student body of nearly three thousand. The college admits to all courses students registered as dyslexic and its admissions policy for such students is under review at the moment. The counselling service will refer students for psychological assessment if they become aware they may have dyslexia while at college.

The college provides a support service for dyslexic students by providing the following:
- Provision of a member of staff to act as a support officer.
- The provision of a computer for lectures and library work.
- The use of a tape recorder in lectures.
- Laptop computers.
- Access to a tutor trained how dyslexia affects students.
- Provision of special courses/study skills seminars.

If necessary, the college will make the following available in exams:
- Use of an amanuensis/scribe.
- Use of a reader.
- The facility to tape exams or take them orally.
- The use of a dictionary, thesaurus or spellmaster.
- Provision of extra time.
- Individual lecturers will be made aware of the student's difficulty.

The college provides information on dyslexia to academic staff and tutor development programmes. The tutor's handbook includes a section on dyslexia. The college also provides information to increase awareness of dyslexia among the student population.

Regional Technical College, Dundalk

There are ten dyslexic students in a student body of over two thousand students.

The college will admit dyslexic students to all courses.
The college provides the following support services:
◆ Photocopying of notes.
◆ Use of a tape recorder in lectures.
◆ A computer for lectures and library work.
◆ Computer facilities such as talking PCs, PC software for dyslexics and magnification systems.
The college will make the following available in exams if necessary:
◆ Use of reader.
◆ Use of a word processor.
◆ The facility to tape exams or take them orally.
◆ The facility to use a dictionary, thesaurus, or spellmaster.
◆ Provision of extra time in exams.
◆ Labelling of scripts so examiners know that a student has dyslexia.

Regional Technical College, Letterkenny

RTC Letterkenny is happy to accept applications from students with special needs, regardless of any physical, sensory or learning disability. Students can choose to indicate their disability, or not, at the application stage. Those who obtain the minimum entry requirements and the appropriate points will be offered a place regardless. The purpose of such revelation therefore is to enable the college to give special consideration to applicants with disability and not to exclude them.

If disabled applicants wish to have their disability taken into consideration at the application stage they should apply as non-standard applicants by checking the appropriate box (box 9, page 3) on the CAO application form. Such applicants should **also** contact the Registrar stating their reasons for requesting special consideration. Where both these actions are taken the applicant will be assessed independently of the points system. Regardless of points, the applicant would usually be required to have achieved minimum entry requirements (5 passes including a pass in either Irish or English and a pass in Maths). However the college may consider waiving this requirement for non-standard applicants. Each such case is reviewed on its own merits. The assessment may include an interview with the Registrar and/or Head of School and it is likely that the college would liaise with the applicant's second-level teachers also. The purpose of such interviews and assessment would be to enable the college satisfy itself that the applicant is capable of undertaking the course of study required. Regardless of whether an applicant has made a disclosure of disability or not at the application stage, the college requests disabled students, who are successful in gaining a place, to notify their Head of School at the earliest opportunity after registration. This is to ensure that arrangements can be put in place to accommodate their needs. Every effort will be made to accommodate such students including, *where budgets allow*, purchase of special equipment.

The college makes the following support services available:
◆ Photocopying of lecture notes can be arranged.
◆ Use of a tape recorder is allowed.
◆ Provision of computer for lectures and library work can be arranged.
◆ Scanners are available to all students on request.

The college makes the following available for exams if necessary:
◆ The facility to tape exams.
◆ Use of a word processor.
◆ The facility to use a dictionary, thesaurus or spellmaster.
◆ Provision on extra time in exams.

Regional Technical College, Limerick

There are currently six dyslexic students attending the college out of a total student body of approximately two thousand seven hundred. The college admits dyslexic students to all courses. Waivers of minimum entry requirements are NOT generally given. Students who wish to be considered for a waiver of minimum entry requirements to a particular course should apply to the College directly (and also to the CAO). The application should include all relevant documentation and assessments. The college makes specific PCs and PC software for dyslexics available.

Regional Technical College, Sligo

There is an incidence of less than 1% of diagnosed dyslexic students in a student body of 2,500. The college admits dyslexic student to all courses. The college would consider waiving the minimum entry requirement. The student should apply as a non-standard applicant on the CAO form. The assessment would take the form of an interview. If the student obtained the minimum entry requirements and points, he/she would automatically be offered a place. While not formally having an assessment policy for students who may become aware of dyslexic difficulties while attending the college, each case would be treated individually.

The college provides the following support services:
◆ Provision of a member of staff to act as support officer.

- Photocopying of lecture notes.
- Use of a tape recorder in exams.

The college provides the following supports if necessary in exams:
- Use of a reader.
- Use of a word processor.
- The facility to tape exams or take them orally.
- The facility to use a dictionary, thesaurus or spellmaster.
- Provision of extra time.

Regional Technical College, Tallaght

The college has approximately 3,000 students including part-time students. Dyslexic students are admitted to all courses. Students can apply as non-standard applicants on the CAO form.

The college provides a support service for dyslexic students which includes:
- The provision of special courses, workshops and study skills seminars for all students.
- Photocopying of lecture notes.
- Use of tape recorder in lectures (with permission).
- All students have access to computing facilities, which include scanners and voice recognition software.

The college makes the following facilities available in exams if necessary:
- Use of amanuensis.
- Use of a reader.
- Use of a word processor.
- The facility to tape exams or take them orally.
- The facility to use a dictionary, thesaurus or spellmaster.
- Provision of extra time in exams.

The college does provide information to increase the awareness of dyslexia among the student body through visiting lecturers and also provides information to all academic staff using E-mail and electronic versions of AHEAD publications.

Regional Technical College, Tralee

There are six identified dyslexic students in a student body of over two and a half thousand. The college admits dyslexic students to all courses. Students should use the non-standard application procedure available through the CAO. Students are assessed for entry individually and do not require necessarily require the maximum points required for entry. The assessment includes an interview and the submission of supporting documentation. The student who applies as a non-standard applicant is offered a place on his/her merits. If a student becomes aware that he/she may have dyslexia while at third level, the college will assist with assessment arrangements and expenses as necessary.

The college provides the following support services, where feasible:

◆ The availability of a member of staff to act as a support officer.
◆ Photocopying of lecture notes.
◆ Use of a tape recorder in exams is under consideration.
◆ Access to a computer for lectures and library work.
◆ The following computer facilities, scanners, talking PCs, PC software for dyslexics and laptops.
◆ Access to a tutor trained in how dyslexia affects students at third-level is under consideration.

The college makes the following available for exams if necessary:

◆ Use of an amanuensis/scribe.
◆ Use of a reader.
◆ Use of a word processor.
◆ The facility to tape exams or take them orally.
◆ The facility to use a dictionary, thesaurus or spellmaster.
◆ The provision on extra time in exams.
◆ Marking of papers by staff trained in dyslexia is being investigated.

The college provides information to increase awareness of dyslexia among students and information on dyslexia to all academic staff as well as staff development programmes. The college will generally be very responsive to student needs once it is advised of these needs and suggest students advise the college of their learning difficulties ahead of registration, so that the necessary facilities and services can be put in place.

Royal College of Surgeons

The college requests dyslexic students, who wish to apply for a place, to contact the college directly.

St Patrick's College, Carlow

The college has a student body of 350 students. The college serves the needs of mildly dyslexic students through its tutorial services. There is no clear policy on accepting students who are severely dyslexic.

St. Patrick's College, Drumcondra

No student diagnosed as dyslexic has attended the college to-date. Admission to the Bachelor of Education is conditional on the medical requirements set out by the Department of Education. Students may apply as non-standard applicants for the Bachelor of Arts degree.

Trinity College Dublin

The college has a number of dyslexic students in a student body of over eleven thousand. The college admits dyslexic students to all courses. The college would consider waiving the minimum entry requirement of a pass grade in a language other than English and students wishing to avail of this waiver should write to the Admissions Officer with appropriate supporting documentation.

The student should indicate dyslexia on pages three and four of the CAO form but points would still be a factor in the allocation of places. If the student applies as a non-standard applicant, he/she will automatically get a place if he/she obtains the points and minimum entry requirements. The college does have an assessment policy for students who become aware they may have dyslexia while at third-level.

The college has a support service and makes the following facilities available:

◆ Provision of a member of staff to act as support officer.
◆ Use of a tape recorder in lectures.
◆ Use of scanners, laptops and talking PCs.

The college makes the following facilities available to dyslexic students if necessary in exams:

◆ Use of an amanuensis/scribe.
◆ Use of a reader.
◆ The facility to tape exams or take them orally.
◆ The facility to use a dictionary, thesaurus or spellmaster.
◆ Provision of extra time in exams.

The college provides information to increase awareness of dyslexia among the student body and to all academic staff.

University College Cork

The college provides a comprehensive support service for students with disabilities with a full-time qualified disability support officer in attendance. The college gives individual support to students according to the each student's needs.

The college is at present (June 1997) preparing a handbook on this service.

University College Dublin

There are twenty-five dyslexic students in a student body of twenty-two thousand.

U.C.D. does not debar dyslexic students from any undergraduate course. In exceptional circumstances the minimum entry requirements may be waived. Such students should apply on page three and four of the CAO form and enclose supporting documentation or alternatively they may submit this documentation directly to the admissions office of the college. Students seeking an exemption from the third language requirement should contact the Registrar of the National University of Ireland with a psychologist's report. Students who apply on page three and four of the CAO form can be assessed independently of the points system. In the case of dyslexic students, assessment is made on an individual basis by the Access Committee. Special category applicants who obtain the points and minimum entry requirements are admitted in the normal way. The college does have an assessment policy for students who have become aware they may have dyslexia while at third-level.

The college provides the following support services:

◆ Provision of a member of staff to act as support officer.
◆ Photocopying of lecture notes.
◆ Use of a tape recorder in lectures.
◆ Provision of a computer for library work.
◆ Provision of scanners, talking PCs, PC software for dyslexics, magnification systems and spellmasters.

The college makes the following available for exams if necessary:

◆ Use of an amanuensis/scribe.
◆ Use of a reader.
◆ Use of a word processor.
◆ The facility to tape exams.
◆ Provision of extra time in exams.
◆ Scripts are labelled so examiners know that the student has dyslexia.

Waterford Institute of Technology

The college has no specific policy on dyslexia. The college welcomes applications from any student with disability. However students should contact the college well in advance to discuss any special requirements that they would have in the event that they were admitted. The college does allow some extra time in exams for students with disability and the disability is kept in mind by the lecturer when correcting scripts.

Add-On Degrees Offered by the Regional Technical Colleges

Appendix

A

Regional Technical College certificate level courses can, in many cases, be the first of three stages on the road to a degree. After completing the certificate and attaining the required grades, the student advances to a one-year diploma. If the student achieves the required grades in the diploma, he can advance to a one-year add-on degree. So in four years (five in the case of engineering) the student will graduate with a degree. All these degrees are fully recognised by the NCEA. It is also possible to transfer to other universities in Ireland and the U.K.

Add-on degrees being offered in the RTC system are:

ATHLONE   Tourism and Hospitality; Software Engineering; Toxicology; Business Studies; Applied Chemistry; Accounting and Finance.

CARLOW   Industrial Biology; Production Technology; Software Engineering; Business Studies; a joint degree programme with the University of Essex in Physics or Chemistry.

CORK   Analytical Chemistry; Biomedical Sciences; Applied Physics and Instrumentation; Structural/Civil Engineering; Fine Art; Applied Social Studies; Ceramics.

DUNDALK   Business Studies; Commercial Computing; Product Design; Building Surveying.

GALWAY   Business Studies; Digital and Software Systems Engineering, Furniture Technology; Software Development; Computer Applications.

LETTERKENNY   Business Studies; Computing.

LIMERICK   Information Technology; Fine Art; Design; Graphics;
               Fashion; Ceramics; Chartered Surveying

SLIGO   Quality Assurance; Engineering; Social Studies;
               Computing; Business Studies; Environmental Science;
               Environmental Chemistry; Occupational Safety.

TALLAGHT   Computing; Business Studies
               (Accounting/Management); Marketing with languages
               (French/German/Spanish/ Japanese); Manufacturing
               Engineering; Applied Chemistry & Biology.

TRALEE   Information Systems Management; Business Studies;
               Computing.

WATERFORD   Business and Financial Studies; Recreation and Leisure;
               Computer Aided Manufacture; Chemistry; Applied
               Social Studies; Legal & Business Studies; Applied
               Biology; Applied Languages; Commercial Software
               Development; Financial Services.

As there is rapid development of these add-on degrees, please consult the
most recent college prospectus.

List of Post Leaving Certificate Colleges

This list includes the main PLC colleges. Further information is available from the Vocational Education Committees in each county.

Dublin
Ballsbridge College, 01-6684806
Ballyfermot Senior College 01-6269421
Colaiste Eanna, Cabra, 01-8389577
St. Kevin's, Clogher Road, 01-4536397
Colaiste Dhulaigh, Coolock, 01-8474399
Crumlin College, 01-4540662
Colaiste Ide, Finglas, 01-8342333
Inchicore Vocational School, 01-4535358
St. Peter's, Killester, 01-8337686
Liberties Vocational School, Dublin 8, 01-4540082
Marino College, Dublin 3, 01-8334201
Pearse College, Dublin 12, 01-4536661
Plunkett College, Whitehall, 01-8371689
Rathmines Senior College, 01-4975334
Ringsend Technical Institute, 01-6684498
Whitehall House Senior College, 01-8376011

College of Commerce, Dundrum, 01-2985412
Dundrum College, 01-2982340
Stillorgan Senior College, 01-2880704
Dun Laoghaire Senior College, 01-2800385
Dun Laoghaire Community College, 01-2809676
Sallynoggin Senior College, 01-2852997

Cavan
College of Further Studies, 049-32633

Carlow
Senior College Carlow, 0503-31187

Cork
Scoil Stiofain Naofa, 021-961020
Scoil Eoin Naofa, 021-276410
School of Commerce, Morrison's Island, 021-270777

Donegal
Letterkenny Vocational School, 074-21047

Galway
Community College, Moinin na gCiseach, 091-755464

Kildare
Kildare College of Further Studies, 045-521287

Kilkenny
Kilkenny Vocational School, 056-22108
Thomastown, Vocational School, 056-24112

Laois
Portlaoise Vocational School, 0502-21480

Limerick
Limerick Senior College, 061-414344

Louth
Drogheda College of Further Education, 041-37105
O Fiaich College, Dundalk, 042-31398

Monaghan
Monaghan Institute of Further Education, 047-84900

Tipperary
Central Technical Institute, Clonmel, 052-21450

Waterford
Central Technical Institute, 051-74053

Westmeath
Moate Business College, 0902-81178

Wicklow
Bray Institute of Further Education, 01-2866233

Private Colleges

The main private colleges include:

American College, Merrion Square, Dublin 2.
  Humanities and Business Studies.
Cork College of Fashion Design, 6 Anglesea Street, Cork.
Dublin Business College, 13-14 Aungier Street, Dublin 2.
  Accounting, Business Studies and Professional Accountancy Bodies Exams.
Griffith College, South Circular Road, Dublin 8. Accounting, Business
  Studies, Computers, Journalism, Business and Law.
Grafton Academy of Dress Design, 6 Herbert Place, Dublin 2.
H.S.I. College, The Crescent, Limerick.
  Marketing, Tourism, Business Studies, Journalism and Computers.
Institute of Public Administration, 57-61 Lansdowne Road, Dublin 4.
  Public Management and Business Studies.
Kilkenny Institute for Higher Education, Ormonde Hall, John's Green,
  Kilkenny.
  Computer Applications, Social Care and Business Studies.
LSB College, 6-9 Balfe Street, Dublin 2.
  Business Studies, Tourism, Psychoanalytical studies, Humanities,
  Anthropology, Accounting, Psychology, Marketing and Languages.
Mid West Business Institute, Rutland St., Limerick.
  Business Studies, Computers, Tourism, Marketing and Accounting.
Montessori Education Centre, 41-43 North Great Georges Street, Dublin 1.
Portobello College, South Richmond Street, Dublin 2.
  Business Studies, Computers, Law and Accountancy.
Portobello School of Child Care, 40 Dominic Street, Dublin 1.
  Child Care, Pre-Nursing, Travel and Tourism and Beauty.

St. Nicholas Montessori College, 16 Adelaide Road, Dun Laoghaire.
School of Practical Childcare, Blackrock, Co. Dublin.
Tiernan Design School, Griffith College, Dublin 8.
  Architectural Draughting, Interior Design.

The Association for Children and Adults with Learning Difficulties

ACLD is a company, limited by guarantee, which is also a registered charity. Founded in 1972 as the Dyslexia Association of Ireland, it aims to promote public awareness of specific learning difficulty and to serve the welfare of people with this difficulty.

The Association lobbies for the provision of appropriate services by the State for all people with dyslexia. It provides an information service to the public, psycho-educational assessment, group and individual tuition for children and adults, teacher training courses, speakers to school and parent groups and organises seminars.

ACLD has twenty branches. It runs twenty-one specialist workshops and four Summer Schools for dyslexic children. It holds six to seven teacher training courses annually. The Association monitors and evaluates new information and teaching methods for the remediation of specific learning difficulty. It keeps in touch with government departments, politicians and relevant professional bodies and educational organisations.

ACLD is a founder member of the European Dyslexia Association, which now has twenty-five member countries. It is also a founder member of Spectrum, an umbrella group of associations for people with hidden learning difficulties. It has long been a corporate member of the British Dyslexia Association, a member of the Disability Federation of Ireland, the Whole Ireland Institute of Special Education and the National Adult Literacy Association. It maintains close links with the Irish National Teachers' Association, the Association of Remedial Teachers of Ireland, the Psychological Association of Ireland and the National Parents' Council.

N.U.I
Matriculation Policy

Policy statement on matriculation requirements for students with learning disabilities affecting language acquisition.

1. The National University of Ireland with its Constituent Universities in Dublin, Cork, Galway and Maynooth is committed to a policy of inclusivity in relation to the admission to the university of students with disabilities and recognises the achievements of the growing numbers of students with disabilities in the university. The NUI has reviewed its matriculation requirements with a view to ensuring that students with certain certifiable learning disabilities, but who in all other respects have the capacity to succeed in higher education, are not excluded from matriculation.

2. The standard matriculation requirements of the National University of Ireland are set out in an annual publication *Minimum Academic Entry and Registration (Matriculation) Requirements*. The NUI recognises that for students with learning difficulties affecting language acquisition, but who in all other respects have the capacity to succeed in higher education, these matriculation requirements may pose particular problems. Attention is drawn to the two special provisions in the current regulations which relate to students with such learning difficulties, as follows:-

◆ Regulation 6.2 (v) permits candidates who have been exempted from Irish at second-level to claim exemption from Irish for matriculation registration purposes. Such exemptions are granted by the NUI on the basis of the Certificates of Exemption from Irish issued by the Department of Education in accordance with Circular M10/94.

◆ Regulation 7 provides a special route to matriculation for students who are professionally certified as having a serious hearing impairment. In such cases, students are exempt from the third language requirement and are permitted to matriculate in six subjects accepted for matriculation purposes, to include Irish or English.

3. The NUI is also prepared to consider applications seeking exemption from the third language requirement from students who are certified by a qualified professional as having a serious dyslexic condition. Such applications are considered on an individual basis. The NUI have been influenced by the Association for Higher Education Access and Disability (AHEAD) in accepting the following definition of dyslexia:-

   ◆ Dyslexia is one of several distinct learning disabilities. It s a specific language-based disorder of constitutional origin characterised by difficulties in single word decoding, usually reflecting insufficient phonological processing. These difficulties in single word decoding are often unexpected in relation to age and other cognitive abilities; they are not the result of generalised development disability or sensory impairment. Dyslexia is manifest by variable difficulty with different forms of language, often including, in addition to problems with reading, a conspicuous problem with acquiring proficiency in writing and spelling.

4. The NUI appreciates that for students aspiring to study at a Constituent University of the National University of Ireland, the matriculation requirements of the university will be a factor in their choice of subjects for the Leaving Certificate. Accordingly, applications for exemption from Irish and/or the third language requirement may be presented to the NUI at any stage following the completion of the Junior Certificate. Applications must be accompanied by a Schools Record Form completed by the Head of School attended. These forms are available from the National University of Ireland, 49 Merrion Square, Dublin 2. Tel: 01-6767246.

5. The NUI emphasises that fulfilling minimum entry requirements is just one step towards registration. Students should also familiarise themselves with the admission requirements of the university to which they intend to apply for admission.

Further Reading

Career Choice 1998, published by Level 3 Publishing and Design, 15 Pembroke St., Dublin 2.

Duddy J. and R. Keane The Student Yearbook and Career Directory, The Student Yearbook Ltd, Shancroft, O'Hanlon Lane, Malahide.

Dunne, R., Applying to College in 1998, Undergraduate Publications Ltd., Rock Cross, Co. Cavan.

Gilroy, D.E. and T.R. Miles, Dyslexia at College, Routledge, 1996.

Hornsby, Dr. B., Overcoming Dyslexia, Optima, 1984.

Jordan, D.R., Dyslexia in the Classroom, Merrill, 1977.

Naughton, M., Dyslexia at Third Level, ACLD, 1995.

Ott, P., How to detect and manage Dyslexia, Heinemann 1997.

Pollock, J. and E. Waller, Day-to-day Dyslexia in the Classroom, Routledge, 1994.

Pumfrey, P. and R., Reason Specific Learning Difficulty (Dyslexia) Challenges and Responses, Routledge 1991.

West, T.G. In the Mind's Eye, Prometheus Books, 1991.

VIDEOS

The Channel 4 Dyslexia video	Produced by Poseidon Film Production. Distributed by Hopeline Video P.O. Box 515 London SW15 6LQ.
How difficult can this be? Understanding Learning Difficulties	Eagle Hill Training Outreach Greenwick, Connecticut. USA.
Lost for Wurds	QED Programme produced by BBC Education Section.
Understanding Dyslexia	The Dyslexia Institute, 133 Gresham Road, Staines, Middlesex TW18 2AJ.

Useful Addresses

AHEAD, 86 St. Stephen's Green, Dublin 2.
ACLD, The Association for Children and Adults with Learning Difficulties. Suffolk Chambers, Suffolk Street, Dublin 2.
Award Systems, 38 Pine Valley Park, Dublin 16.
An Bord Altranais, 31-32 Fitzwilliam Street, Dublin 2.
The British Council, 22 Mount Street, Dublin 2.
The British Dyslexia Association, 98 London Road, Reading, Berks RG1 5AU.
CAO, Central Admissions Office, Tower House, Eglington Street, Galway.
CERT, CERT House, Amiens Street, Dublin 1.
The Dyslexia Computer Resource Centre, Department of Psychology, University of Hull, Hull HU6 7RX.
ETC Consult, 17 Leeson Park, Dublin 6.
Gaisce, The President's Award, Block H, Dublin Castle, Dublin 2.
Interactive Services Ltd., Unit 25 Phibsboru Pl., Dublin 7.
Kinesiology Institute, 84 Cappaghmore Road, Clondalkin, Dublin 22.
National Training and Development Institute, Roslyn Park, Beach Road, Sandymount, Dublin 4.
Scotopic Sensitivity, Ms. M. McGready, 14 Chalet Gardens, Lucan, Co. Dublin.
SKILL, 336 Brixton Road, London L 2W9 7AA.
Teagasc, 19 Sandymount Avenue, Dublin 4.
UCAS, Fulton House, Jessop Avenue, Cheltenham, Glouchestershire, GLE 503 35H.
Youth Information Offices in local areas.

Index

119